CIRCUMFERENCE

POETRY IN TRANSLATION

AUTUMN | WINTER 2003

CIRCUMFERENCE
Volume 1, Issue 1 · Autumn/Winter 2003
© 2003 CIRCUMFERENCE, Inc.
ISBN: 0-9743863-08
Please visit our website at *www.circumferencemag.com*.

EDITORS
Stefania Heim
Jennifer Kronovet

DESIGNER
Daniel Beraca Visel
LANGUAGE EXPERT
Kevin Herwig
WEB DESIGN
St-Eve.com

ADVISORY BOARD
Joshua Beckman
Caroline Crumpacker
Richard Howard
Brett Fletcher Lauer
J.P. Seaton
Rosmarie Waldrop
Eliot Weinberger

CIRCUMFERENCE is a sponsored project of the New York Foundation for the Arts (NYFA), a 501(c)(3), tax-exempt organization.

To subscribe please make checks payable to **CIRCUMFERENCE**. Subscriptions are $15 per year (two issues). Single-copy price is $10.

When submitting work, please send five or six translated poems along with the originals and a self-addressed, stamped envelope.

To become a HERO ($100) or FRIEND ($40) of **CIRCUMFERENCE** and help sustain this journal, please make all checks payable to our fiscal sponsor, NYFA, and mail to our P.O. Box, below. All donations are fully tax-deductible to the extent provided by law.

Mail all material to:

CIRCUMFERENCE
P.O. Box 27
New York, New York 10159-0027

Contents

바깥에 관한 반가사유

해 속의 검은 장수하늘소여
눈먼 것은 성스러운 병이다

활어관 밑바닥에 엎드려 있는 넙치,
짐자전거 지나가는 바깥을 본다, 보일까

어찌하겠는가, 깨달았을 때는
모든 것이 이미 늦었을 때
알지만 나갈 수 없는, 無窮의 바깥;
저무는 하루, 문 안에서 검은 소가 운다

HWANG JI-WOO

Sitting Cross-legged and Thinking about the World Outside

A black longicorn beetle under the sun—
blindness is a sacred disease!

A flatfish lying on the bottom of the tank
looks outside at a bike passing, carrying goods. Can it see?

What can it do? It's already too late,
it understands the situation.

It sees the world outside—unlimited, impassable space.
The day wanes. A black ox weeps inside the door.

translated from Korean by
WON-CHUNG KIM & CHRISTOPHER MERRILL

대답 없는 날들을 위하여 2

갈 봄 여름 없이, 처형받은 세월이었지
축제도 화환도 없는 세월이었지
그 세월 미처 날뛰고 맹목의 세례식—

개나리꽃 옆에서 우리는
물벼락 맞았지 진달래꽃 앞에서
눈물 벼락 맞고, 우리는 國籍을 잃고
우리는 이데올로기의 色盲이 되고
자욱한 연기, 질식할 것 같은 철쭉꽃 뒤에서
몰지각한 망상주의자
망상주의자였지 우리는, 연방 기침하면서 불순한
　사대주의자,
위험한 이상주의자였지 손 한번 들어올리지 못하고
소리 한번 못 지르고 우리는,
한 다발 두 다발 문밖으로 들려나가는 모습들을
'느린 그림'으로 지켜보는
들뜬 회의주의자, 혼수 상태의 세월이었지

HWANG JI-WOO

For the Unanswered Days II

Regardless of the season, these were the condemned days,
days without festivals or wreathes,
mad days when the baptism of blindness ran wild—

By the forsythia blossoms, we were
doused; by the azalea blossoms
we were tear gassed. We lost
our nationality, we went color blind to ideology.
Behind the dense fog and suffocating royal azaleas
we turned into paranoid babblers.
Indeed we were paranoid, we were lying flunkies who coughed and coughed.
Dangerous ideologues who could neither raise our hands
nor even let out a cry.
Restless skeptics who watched "in slow motion"
pictures of us carried away in bundles.
These were the comatose days.

translated from Korean by
WON-CHUNG KIM & CHRISTOPHER MERRILL

沿 革

섣달 스무아흐레 어머니는 시루떡을 던져 앞 바다
의 흩어진 물결들을 달래었습니다. 이튿날 내내 靑
苔밭 가득히 찬비가 몰려왔습니다. 저희는 雨期의
처마 밑을 바라볼 뿐 가난은 저희의 어떤 관례와도
같았습니다. 滿潮를 이룬 저의 가슴이 무장무장 숨
가빠하면서 무명옷이 젖은 저의 一家의 심한 살냄새
를 맡았습니다. 빠른 물살들이 土房門을 빠져나가는
소리를 들으며 저희는 낮은 沿岸에 남아 있었습니다
모든 近景에서 이름없이 섬들이 멀어지고 늦게 떠
난 木船들이 그 사이에 오락가락했습니다. 저는 바
다로 가는 대신 뒤안 장독의 작게 부서지는 파도 소
리를 들었습니다. 빈 항아리마다 저의 아버님이 떠
나신 솔섬 새울음이 그치질 않았습니다. 물 건너 어
느 계곡이 깊어가는지 차라리 귀를 막으면 南蠻의
멀어져가는 섬들이 세차게 울고울고 하였습니다.
어머니는 저를 붙들었고 內地에는 다시 연기가 피
어올랐습니다. 그럴수록 近視의 겨울 바다는 눈부신
저의 눈시울에서 여위어갔습니다. 아버님이 끌려가
신 날도 나루터 물결이 저렇듯 잠잠했습니다. 물가
에 서면 가끔 지친 물새떼가 저의 어지러운 무릎까
지 밀려오기도 했습니다. 저는 어느 외딴 물나라에
서 흘러들어온 흰 상여꽃을 보는 듯했습니다. 꽃 속
이 너무나 환하여 저는 빨리 잠들고 싶었습니다. 언
뜻언뜻 어머니가 잠든 胎夢중에 아버님이 드나드시
는 것이 보였고 저는 石花밭을 넘어가 燐光의 밤바
다에 몰래 그물을 넣었습니다. 아버님을 태운 상여
꽃이 끝없이 끝없이 새벽물을 건너가고 있습니다.
朔望 바람이 불어왔습니다. 그러나 바람 속은 저
의 死後처럼 더 이상 바람 소리가 나지 않고 木船들
이 빈 채로 돌아왔습니다. 해초 냄새를 피하여 새들
이 저의 무릎에서 뭍으로 날아갔습니다. 물가 사람
들은 머리띠의 흰 천을 따라 內地로 가고 여인들은
還生을 위해 저 雨期의 靑苔밭 넘어 再拜三拜 흰떡
을 던졌습니다. 저는 괴로워하는 바다의 內心으로
내려가 땅에 붙어 괴로워하는 모든 물풀들을 뜯어
올렸습니다.
內陸에 어느 나라가 망하고 그 대신 자욱한 앞바
다에 때아닌 배추꽃들이 떠올랐습니다. 먼 훗날 제
가 그물을 내린 子宮에서 燐光의 항아리를 건져올
사람은 누구일까요.

HWANG JI-WOO

History

On the 29th of December, my mother threw steamed rice cakes into the sea in front of our house and smoothed its scattered waves. The next day a cold rain poured onto the laver field. We only looked into the eaves of the rainy spell: poverty was our custom. My heart at high tide worked harder, my cotton clothes carried the stench of my family's wet flesh. Hearing the current swiftly ebbing from the front yard, we remained at the lower seashore.

The unnamed islands moved far from view, and the wooden boats that left the pier late sailed back and forth between them. Instead of entering the sea, I listened to the sound of waves breaking over the jar stand in the back yard. In the empty jars the cries of the birds of Sol Island, from which my father left, never stopped. When I could no longer hear which valley across the water deepened, the receding southern bays cried bitterly over and over.

My mother wouldn't let me go out, and in the interior the smoke fluttered again. The myopic winter sea was thinning at the sparkling edge of my eyes. When my father was dragged from the house, the waves at the ferry were as calm as this. If I stood by the shore, flocks of exhausted water birds would be shoved into my dizzy knees. To me, they looked like white funeral flowers flown in from some remote island. The corollas of the flowers were so bright I wished I could fall asleep. In a flash I saw my father coming and going in my mother's dream of conception, and I crossed the oyster flats and hurled nets into the phosphorescent night sea. The flowers decorating my father's bier were endlessly crossing the early morning sea.

The wind that blows every half month raged. But the wind had no sound of the wind, like my body after death; the wooden ships returned empty. To avoid the smell of the seaweed, the birds flew from my knees to the interior. The people near shore followed the white cloth of their headbands and moved inland, while the women bowed two and three times for their reincarnation, throwing steamed rice cakes into the field of laver in a rainy season. I dived into the heart of the writhing sea and pulled out all the ailing seaweed living on the bottom.

A country collapsed in the interior and cabbages floated on the dense sea. I wonder who will eventually haul up the phosphorescent jar from the womb into which I hurled my net.

translated from Korean by
WON-CHUNG KIM & CHRISTOPHER MERRILL

Ceremonia en una Basílica

Ya no tengo edad para cuidarme.
Necesito qué necesito, además de nada?
Salir de risotadas con mi amigo que murió.
Tirar las pesadillas como papel picado
desde la azotea del último día.

Si hay otra vida yo ya estoy ahí,
con las grandes pasiones que el hígado consintió.
Con una tía loca que nos enseñaba catecismo
y un día se hartó de nuestras risas y con Dios
que tambien "se puso el sombrero y se fue."

Un curriculum en ayunas para poder salir del pais,
al pie de la escalerilla del vacío.
Edad?
Desde Siempre.
Sexo?
Una cruz.
Nacionalidad?
Un karma.
Me voy porque no quiero.
Me quedo porque es lo único.
Y porque la palabra es gratis.

FERNANDO SÁNCHEZ SORONDO

Ceremony in a Basilica

I'm already too old to care for myself.
I need—what do I need, besides nothing?
To go on laughing with my friend who died.
To throw nightmares like confetti
from the flat roof of the last day.

If there's another life, beyond, I'm already there:
with the grand passions the liver allowed,
and a mad aunt who taught us catechism
and got fed up one day with our laughter, and with God
who also "put on his *sombrero* and left."

A curriculum of fasts, a way to leave the country,
at the foot of the stepladder of the abyss. Age?
As of always. Sex? A cross. Nationality?
Karma. I'm going because I don't want to. I stay
because this is all there is. And because words are gratis.

translated from Spanish by
IDRA NOVEY

एकत्रासनसङ्गतिः परिहृता प्रत्युद्गमाहूरत-

स्ताम्बूलानयनच्छलेन रभसाश्लेषो ऽपि संविघ्नितः ।

आलापो ऽपि न मिश्रितः परिजनं व्यापारयन्त्यान्तिके

कान्तं प्रत्युपचारतश्चतुरया कोपः कृतार्थीकृतः ॥ १७ ॥

काञ्च्या गाढतराववद्धवसनप्रान्ता किमर्थं पुनर्

मुग्धाक्षी स्वपितीति तत्परिजनं स्वैरं प्रिये पृच्छति ।

मातः सुप्तिमपीह लुम्पति ममेत्यारोपितक्रोधया

पर्यस्य स्वपनच्छलेन शयने दत्तो ऽवकाशस्तया ॥२०॥

AMARU

Amarusataka 17

Rising to greet him—
still far off—
she avoided sharing a couch.
When he reached for her
off she ran for betel nut leaf.
Nor could he speak to her
so diligent was she
to the servants' instructions.
Shrewd girl, every courtesy
applied just
to get back at him.

Amarusataka 20

Why is this enchanted
creature asleep,
a sash fastened over her robe—?
He was softly querying
the servants
when she cried bitterly
Mother, he disrupts my dreams even here!
and turned as if
sleeping to make room
on the bed.

translated from Sanskrit by
ANDREW SCHELLING

प्रातः प्रातरुपागतेन जनिता निर्निन्दिता चक्षुषोर्

मन्दाया मम गौरवव्यपनयादुत्पादितं लाघवं ।

किं मुग्धेन कृतं त्वया मरणभीर्मुक्ता मया गम्यतां

दुःखं तिष्ठसि यच्च पथ्यमधुना कर्तास्मि तच्छ्रोष्यसि ॥३०॥

स्वं दृष्ट्वा करजक्षतं मधुमदक्षीबाविचार्येर्ष्यया

गच्छन्ती क्व नु गच्छसीति विधृता बाला पटान्ते मया ।

प्रत्यावृत्तमुखी सबाष्पनयना सा मुञ्च मुञ्चेति मां

कोपप्रस्फुरिताधरं यदवदत् तत्केन विस्मार्यते ॥ ४७ ॥

AMARU

16

Amarusataka 30

Dawn after dawn
our lovemaking
took the sleep from my eyes.
A weight lifted.
For once my heart felt light.
Now what have you done?
Go . . . you are foolish & miserable
and death no longer scares me.
One day you may hear
which path
I've decided to take.

Amarusataka 47

We'd been drinking.
She noticed wounds on my skin
from her own
fingernails
and bolted up jealously.
Let go, she cried when I caught her skirt.
Tear-streaked face averted
lower lip quavering—
who could forget
   what she said next?

translated from Sanskrit by
ANDREW SCHELLING

Ja Sam Staromodna Cura

Ja sam staromodna cura,
Volim kuće prizemljuše krastavih zidova
Sa dvorištima krcatim starudijama,
Umesto oblakodera i apartmana
U kojima se budim i spavam.
Muškatle u prozorima i u loncima na tufne
Više volim od imitacija, od «veštaka».
Ja sam staromodna cura,
Što više voli vespe umesto automobila.
Tamndrkanje tramvaja i kloparanje parnjače,
Više od zvižduka mlaznjaka,
Puteljke umesto avenija i bulevara,
Kojima moje potpetice odzvanjaju.
Ja sam staromodna cura,
Što voli miris opranog veša
Koga vetar naduvava
Do moga lica, preko moga nosa,
I sve ono što veje iz prethodnog života.
Ja sam staromodna cura,
Još slušam longplejke i tipkam na *Olivetti*.
Govorim hvala, izvinite, molim.
Volim da mi dasa pripali cigaretu,
Otvori vrata, pridrži kaput, primakne stolicu,
Da me svlači krpicu po krpicu.
Ja sam staromodna cura,
Što voli kič scene sa zalascima sunca,
Modne žurnale i porodične albume,
Od okretnih igara «stiskavac» jedino razumem.
Nove filmove još gledam na stari način,
Iz zadnjeg reda bioskopske polutame,
Vežbajući «francuski poljubac».
Ja sam staromodna cura,
Ne zujim i ne skitaram kojekuda,
U kući dreždim povazdan,
Kao glineni ćup sušeći se na promaji
Samoće i zadovoljstava,
Mamurna od snova.
Ja sam staromodna cura
Sto se kuva u sopstvenom loncu
Marke hoću-neću.
O ljubavi i strasti malo šta znam,
Devičijeg srca rođena udovica,

(continued)

I'm an Old-Fashioned Girl

I'm an old-fashioned girl.
I like low houses with pock-marked walls
With yards full of junk
Instead of skyscrapers and apartment houses
Where I wake and sleep.
Geraniums on windowsills in polka-dot cans,
I prefer to artificial flowers.
I'm an old-fashioned girl,
That likes a scooter better than an automobile,
The rattle of a street car,
The rumble of a steam locomotive,
More than a whistle of a jet.
Footpaths instead of avenues and boulevards
Where my heels go clicking.
I'm an old-fashioned girl,
That likes the smell of clean laundry
The wind brings to my face, over my nose,
Everything that falls like snow in my previous life.
I'm an old-fashioned girl,
I still listen to long playing records
And type on an Olivetti.
I say thank you, please excuse me.
I like when a gentlemen gives me light,
Opens the door for me,
Holds my coat, offers me a chair.
And takes my clothes off garment by garment.
I'm an old-fashioned girl,
That likes kitsch landscapes with sunsets,
Fashion magazines and family albums.
Close dancing is the only kind I understand.
I watch the new movies in the old way
Sitting in the half-dark,
Practicing French-kissing in the last row.
I'm an old-fashioned girl,
I don't go buzzing around
I'm always to be found at home
Like a clay pot drying in the draft
Of solitude and contentment,
Hangover from all the dreaming.
I'm an old-fashioned girl,
That's cooking in her own casserole
Called I-want-I-don't-want.

(continued)

Pod čijim nogama život kulja
Kao para iz šahta
Koju zaobilazim brzim koracima.
Ja sam staromodna cura,
Ne kupujem po sniženoj ceni
Ni osmehe ni svilu.
Ne nosim mini suknje i dekoltee,
Bilo bi to lako oružje za nekog
Ko je nameran da osvaja bez.
Ja sam staromodna cura
Niti psujem, niti zvocam, niti besnim,
Možete me mazati na hleb.
Al s medom se uvek dobije malo otrova,
Ljubavi u smrtonosnim dozama.
Ja sam staromodna cura,
Stari momak žulja me kao nova cipela,
Koju moram izuti, zameniti.
Za jednog udobnog kao patika,
Ili razgaženog kao susetkin muž.
Ja sam staromodna cura,
Dobra prema muškarcima,
Kao prema onima koji se plaše mraka,
Lifta i prelaska ulice van pešačkog prelaza.
Ja sam staromodna cura,
Drevna kao Kartagina,
Minimalno oštećena zubom vremena.
Muzejski komad koga nema na aukciji.
Pipanje nije dozvoljeno.
Uzmi ili ostavi!

RADMILA LAZIC

20

I know little about love and passion,
A widow born with a virgin's heart
Under whose feet life pours out
Like steam out of a manhole
Which I avoid with my quick steps.
I'm an old-fashioned girl,
I buy nothing at bargain rates,
Neither smiles nor rolls of silk.
I don't wear mini skirts and low cut dresses
To make it easy for whoever
Wants to steal a kiss.
I'm an old-fashioned girl.
I don't cuss, complain or rage.
You can spread me on your toast,
Although honey always comes with a bit of poison,
Love in fatal doses
I'm an old-fashioned girl,
My old boyfriend pinches me like a new shoe
Which I need to take off, replace
With someone as comfortable as a slipper,
Or broken in like my neighbor's husband.
I'm an old-fashioned girl,
Nice to all the guys
As I am to all those who are afraid of the dark,
Afraid of elevators
And crossing the street where it's not allowed.
I'm an old-fashioned girl,
As ancient as Carthage,
Minimally damaged by the tooth of time.
A museum piece that is not at auction.
Touching is not permitted.
Take it or leave it!

translated from Serbian by
CHARLES SIMIC

tiraa de **Secundum Lüna**

VII

Oh bel belé, perla-livàster ögg,
suspir de verla...
Ciallâd de semper, nient che nu' sia fàrfar,
ma, 'stess del cioll, che la matina s'arsa e dis
«... el sû... oh dí cumenzià... un tram... i vus... »
Paròl antigh. Ma dím, làer sgarzèl che sa,
sé g'û de dít? che ciel g'û d'inventàm?
«... la nott, el dí... la pas, la guèra... i mort... »
Croda l'ütünn, la lüna la se sbianca,
dora l'estâ che primavera cascia,
che l'omm l'è fjö di strepp che dà i balòres
per crèss, slungàss, müdàss... 'n òrghen... 'na pianta...
ma 'l püresín de scrutta restarà.
I verb în müff, paròl d'amur fan üsma.
Ma 'l sentiment l'è 'l fiur d'un òmm bardassa,
che, se dis ciau, le dis per sua beltâ.

IX

Se strüsa a spass un mort, sí, nüm, de cera,
nel grev garbüj che dren'l'è 'n scalvascià,
balchèm la libertâ 'me 'na bandera
che, sbrega, gussa un négher spegasciâ.
Ghív no pagüra, òmm, de la suverna!
e baffi! de la brügna di peccâ...
La mort l'è inamuràss, e, 'me d'inverna,
stà a la fenestra a vedè fiuccà.

(continued)

from **Secundum Lüna**

VII

Hey pretty play-thing, pearl olive eyes,
shrike's sigh...
It's the same old mutter-junk, thin-whisped lies,
some asshole, who wakes in the morning, and says:
"the sun... oh day to begin... a tram... voices..."
Ancient words. You, young, all-knowing lip, tell me:
what words do I have to say? what sky do I have to invent?
"the night... the day... times of peace, the war... the dead..."
Autumn crumbles with falling leaves,
the moon turns to snow, and summer,
sprouting forth from spring, gilds golden.

And yes, all men are sons to spurting youth's tugs
to grow, stretch tall, change shape
... as hollow seeds... or garden plants...
But do not fear: the hen's hatched chick will remain.

The verbs are full of mold, and the words of love stink rotten.
And yet, emotion is the flower of the artless man
who bestows his rare hello upon others
only in order to create his own, selfless, beauty.

IX

We haul a dead man into motion, yes, we of wax,
in his knotted tangle that breaks inside,
we labor liberty like a flag full of wind
that rips and drips scribbled ink.
But men, do not fear the broken earth!
and breathe easy! about those mortuary chambers of sins...

To die is to fall in love,
to stand, wintertime, by the window,
and watch the snow fall.

(continued)

XXVIII

Avissi, mí, l'amur, cum' una tuss
de pelabròcch, o 'n zerbinòtt cun l'üga,
o quj ganassa ch'j sburra 'me che füss
'na fonna ingual a l'oltra, o 'na carüga
che sbava in due la passa i sò smanièss,
o'n quaj cunílli ch'a fà fjö mandrüga,
ma g'û 'n amur che vegn da quj sciurèss
due 'l fràgur d'una man el te spaüra
e se 'na man le tucca... oh strabelèss!
Ma 'me l'è müt quel ciel! e l'aria scüra!
Avissi mí 'n amur sensa dulur...

XXXII

« ... e quindi uscimmo a riveder le stelle ».
E sí, olter che stell, anca i cujun
destorbia j öcc e se ne véd de bèlle,
quan' dal nòbel pian 'na quaj tubusa
la cicca un bâs, e 'n para de puppèj
per un buttun canàja j se scamisa...
El cialanun el s'era smentegâ di dorisdej!
Ch'j òmm în là e, ch'j cialla, ch'j se sfrisa,
tanfosgna, spessigotta, van fasnèj,
e sí ch'în semper là e, a la barbisa,
l'è assé vulzà un öcc, e sü de birulèj!
Ch'andarí in barca, farí fadiga aj rèm,
ma quan' zaquâ, 'na stella, sü nel cel
la vardarí 'me mai, e 'sti sberlèff del mar
cuntra la chiglia, e bev quèl'aria,
e de la stella sentarí el sò fiâ,
e no, i mè òmm!, par squasi che la barca
due la s'insogna la poda pü turnà.

XXXVI

Secundum lüna u secundum bírgum,
pussíbel l'impussíbel par che sia,
'na donna che del cel la par 'na vírgum
de terra e crüdeltâ la fantasia

(continued)

24

XXVIII

Would that I had love, like the dry cough
of the branch-bark peeler, or the sugar-greased dandy,
or the thick-jowled prince, whose bottomless water-well
comes for all women alike,
or of the slug,
who drools its slime
where it drops its cravings,
or the garden hare, who chewing its cud,
breeds forth its litter,
but, as it is, though, I've got love
that's born from an urbanity that fears the fragile hand,
and should that hand brush by . . . oh, poor man's drop of sweet red wine!
But how the sky stands mute! And how the air hangs dark!
Would that I had love without suffering . . .

XXXII

" , , , e quindi uscimmo a rivedere le stele" (Dante, *Inferno*)

And yes, forget about stars, also men's balls
unfog eyes and see all sorts of crazy things,
when from the noble floor some Tobosa slut or other
spits down a kiss and a pair of unripe melons,
undressing for an undone button . . .
And to think the charlatan had forgotten about beautiful women!
'Cause the men are there, chattering, clawing past one another,
rummaging, pinching, bewitched, and yet,
they're always there, eyes fixed on woman-fur,
it's enough to raise an eye, and there, twenty centimeters up!
Men, men, once imprisoned, you escape yourselves as enemies,
hey, wet your beaks! and raise your rods!
For you'll all set out to sea, and struggle with the oars,
and, laying down, look up, dazzled, by a shining star.
As the waves roll by, and toss their spray against the keel,
you drink the air, and feel the star's close breath,
and woah, dear men!
'fraid that after all, this old ship
is dreams away.

XXXVI

According to the moon or according to foolish superstition,
possibly the impossible is indeed possible,
a woman, from the sky, who appears a virgin
soils your imagination with mud and cruelty, and wounds you   *(continued)*

te spurca e la te sbrega la fullia
d'un làvur, d'un tremà...Malincunia
de vèss camüff e impurâ d'arlía!
Che mai l'amur capíss 'st'imputacciada
due 'l dulur l'è nient e te risía
quel fiur de la memoria sburdasciada,
e den' la smerg, la se gringa, e raffa
un lengujnö, un quaj lenscín de nada,
ma 'l sacrusant che sia un sogn de smaffa
e minga vera 'sto sprellàsc tasè,
ch'a l'aria ferma 'riva 'me 'na s'giaffa
e tí né piang te pòdet né savè...
Oh, dím del feng! dím de la busía!
dím che 'n giögh, un ghign, divertiment,
oh amur, che forsi a 'n olter muraría,
dím che per mí t'é pruâ mai nient.

LIV

Medan d'un trunch sun chí, che bütti mal,
ch'i frund el vent je möv di mè penser,
ma 'l cör... Oh cör smarî, 'me 'n oss de garla,
de legna fâ, d'i amur e dal sugnà,
te síghet! Nissün sent. El busch caragna,
e i tò ravís la terra magnarà...
Oh tí, che mí t'û dâ la mia tampesta,
se neghi, sí, te slúnghet la tua man,
ma per tegním, cume d'un òmm ch'impesta,
trí méter, mezza terra, püssé in là.

FRANCO LOI

with the madness of lips, of a single quiver . . . Sad shame,
to be lured and undone by the imaginary!
Love will never understand this soggy mess,
where sorrow is nothing, and eats away
at memory's mud-spattered flower,
which crawls inside, and squirms,
and writhes, and steals
the slender tongue, the worthless junk-bent hook you'd hid.
And nothing in all this is really clear, save the absolute certainty
that this is a trickster-dream, and that this heavy silence,
striking the still air like a hollow slap,
is kept for no real reason.

And you, unable to cry, unable to understand . . .
Oh, talk to me about pretending! Talk to me about lies!
Tell me it was a game, a good laugh, a good time, oh,
love, perhaps ready to die for someone else,
tell me, for once, that you've never given a damn
for me.

LIV

Like some tree log, I sit here, badly sprouting,
wind tossing the branches of my thoughts, but this heart . . .
Oh, heart, bewildered, like the bark's bone,
made of wood, from countless lovers, countless dreams,
you screech! Yet no one heeds you.
The wood cries endless, and the soil eats your roots . . .
Hey you, to whom I gave my storm, if I should drown,
perhaps, you would stretch out your hand,
but to hold my body as one holds the body
of a man sick with the plague:
three meters, half the world, or could you slide just a bit
further away?

translated from Milanese by
GIULIANA CHAMEDES

Çekişme

Alışılmamışı bulmak istiyor,
alışılmışı getiriyor oysa yaşam.
Sürekli bir çekişme, öbürü diretiyor.
Sonunda öpüp başına koyuyor gelenleri,
kuş cıvıltısı dalda, kararmış yasemin ağızlık,
parlayan cam kırığı gibi şeyler otların arasında,
kimi gün beylik bir düşünce, alabildiğine gündelik.
Elleri böğründe, küskün, gözleri yerde:
—Haklısın, diyor, sen haklısın, her zaman olduğu gibi.

OKTAY RİFAT

Conflict

He wants to discover the unaccustomed,
but life keeps bringing the accustomed to him.
A constant tug of war, the other one resists.
Finally he embraces all the things that come to him,
birds twittering on the branch, a darkened jasmine mouthpiece,
things like glittering shards among the weeds,
some days a commonplace idea, belonging all the way to this day.
Helpless, his hands tied, sullen, he stands, looking down:
"You are right," he says. "You are right, as always."

translated from Turkish by
TALAT HALMAN

extrait de **Fragments d'une genèse oubliée**

20

Je te connais bien mon frère

Nous nous sommes rencontrés souvent au fil des épreuves

La première fois, c'est le tortionnaire qui nous a présentés l'un à l'autre. Même avec le bandeau sur les yeux, nous nous sommes reconnus. Puis je t'ai entendu crier, crier, et j'avais hâte de prendre ta place, d'offrir ma chair à l'insupportable qui vrillait ta chair.
Plus tard, nous nous sommes retrouvés dans l'attente. Le mur qui nous séparait était si friable. Nous en avons fait un cahier de musique. Chaque nuit, nous échangions de sobres partitions:
—Qu'as-tu mangé
—Que lis-tu
—As-tu reçu une lettre
—Qu'as-tu vu dans la lune
—Le moineau à la patte cassée t'a-t-il rendu visite
—L'aimée a-t-elle répandu du parfum sur ton oreiller? Lilas ou jasmine? Musc ou ambre?

Parfois je t'entendais crier dans ton sommeil et je revivais la scène. Toi ou moi, aux prises avec la forme et son ombre. Ta poitrine ou la mienne ouverte par un rat-chirurgien fouillant dans nos viscères, cherchant on aurait dit à extirper notre âme.

Bien plus tard, c'est dans un désert glacial que nous nous sommes croisés. Un écran de neige nous séparait, et nous avions du mal à trouver belle la neige. Ta bouche nommait l'exil avant d'être scellée. Et sur tes yeux, je voyais palpiter le papillon de la dernière image. Une terrasse blanche où pousse cette plante aux fleurs jaunes appelées "crottes de chat". Faute de maison, une terrasse chaulée où flotte le linge de l'enfance telles les voiles du prodigieux navire.

Je te connais bien mon frère
et tu me connais
aussi bien que la poche lourde
aqueuse
de ta tête

Alors
tends-moi la main
donne-moi la clé
dont tu n'as que faire

ABDELLATIF LAÂBI

from **Fragments of a forgotten genesis**

20

Brother, I know you well

We often met in the passing trials

The torturer introduced us. Even blindfolded we recognized each other. Then I heard you cry and cry, and I hurried to take your place, offering my flesh to the unbearable that pierced your flesh.
Later, we met again in expectation. The wall separating us crumbled. There we composed our musical notebook. Each night we exchanged notes from the sober score:
—What have you eaten
—What have you read
—Did you receive a letter
—What did you see in the moon
—Has the sparrow with the broken leg returned
—Did your lover spill some perfume on your pillow? Lilac or jasmine? Musk or amber?

Sometimes I heard you cry in your sleep and I relived the scene. You or me, grappling with the form and its shadow. Your breast or mine opened by a rat-surgeon digging in our intestines, searching, we said to extirpate our souls.

Much later, we ran across each other in an icy desert. A screen of snow separated us and we had trouble finding the snow beautiful. You mouthed *exile* before your mouth was sealed shut. And in your eyes, I saw the beating butterfly of the last image. A white floor on which this plant with yellow flowers called "crottes de chat." Lacking a house, a whitewashed floor on which the linen of childhood floated like a prodigious ship.

Brother, I know you well
and you know me
as well as the heavy
aqueous pocket
of your head

So
hold out your hand
give me the key
it's all you can do

translated from French by
GORDON HADFIELD & NANCY HADFIELD

aus *Zyklus III,* **Lichtzwang**

WURFSCHEIBE, mit
Vorgesichten besternt,

wirf dich

aus dir hinaus.

from Cycle III of **Lightduress**

D<small>ISCUS</small>, bestarred
with face fronts,

throw yourself

out of yourself.

KLOPF die
Lichtkeile weg:

das schwimmende Wort
hat der Dämmer.

Knock the
lightwedges off:

dusk's got
the swimming word.

DIE ENTSPRUNGENEN
Graupapageien
lesen die Messe
in deinem Mund.

Du hörts regnen
und meinst, auch diesmal
sei's Gott.

THE ESCAPED
gray parrots
say mass
in your mouth.

You hear it rain
and guess that this time too
it's God.

IN DEN DUNKELSCHLÄGEN erfuhr ichs:

du lebst auf mich zu, dennoch,
im Steigrohr,
im
Steigrohr.

IN THE DARK CLEARINGS I learned it:

you live toward me, nevertheless,
in the standpipe,
in the
standpipe.

SCHNEID DIE GEBETSHAND
aus
der Luft
mit der Augen-
schere,
kapp ihre Finger
mit deinem Kuß:

Gefaltetes geht jetzt
atemberaubend vor sich.

CUT THE PRAYERHAND
from
the air
with the eye-
scissors,
lop off its fingers
with your kiss:

the folded now happens
breathtakingly.

Ich kann dich noch sehen: ein Echo,
ertastbar mit Fühl-
wörtern, am Abschieds-
grat.

Dein Gesicht scheut leise,
wenn es auf einmal
lampenhaft hell wird
in mir, an der Stelle,
wo man am schmerzlichsten Nie sagt.

PAUL CELAN

I CAN STILL SEE YOU: an echo,
palpable with feel-
words, at the parting-
ridge.

Your face shies quietly,
when all at once
lamplike it lights up
in me, at the place
where most painfully one says Never.

translated from German by
PIERRE JORIS

過故融公蘭若

池上青蓮宇　林間白馬泉　故人成異物　過客獨潛

然　旣禮新松塔　還尋舊石筵　平生竹如意　猶挂草

堂前

At Lumen-Empty Monastery, Visiting the Hermitage of Master Jung, My Departed Friend

The blue-lotus roof standing beside a pond,
White-Horse Creek tumbling through forests,

and my old friend some strange thing now.
A lingering visitor, alone and grief-stricken

after graveside rites among pines, I return,
looking for your sitting-mat spread on rock.

Bamboo that seems always my own thoughts:
it keeps fluttering here at your thatch hut.

translated from Chinese by
DAVID HINTON

寄趙正字

正字芸香閣幽人竹葉園經過宛如昨歸臥寂無
喧高鳥能擇木羝羊漫觸藩物情今已見從此願
忘言

MENG HAO-JAN

Sent to Ch'ao, the Palace Reviser

You polish words in rue-scented libraries,
and I live in bamboo-leaf gardens, a recluse

wandering each day the same winding path
home to rest in the quiet, no noise anywhere.

A bird soaring the heights chooses its tree,
but the hedge soon tangles impetuous goats.

Today, things seen becoming thoughts felt:
this is where you start forgetting the words.

translated from Chinese by
DAVID HINTON

登望楚山最高頂

山水觀形勝　襄陽美會稽
最高惟望楚　曾未一攀躋
石壁疑削成　衆山比全低
晴明試登陟　目極無端倪
雲夢掌中小　武陵花處迷
暝還歸騎下　蘿月在深溪

MENG HAO-JAN

Climbing Long-View Mountain's Highest Peak

Rivers and mountains beyond the form seen:
Hsiang-yang's beauty brings them in reach,

and Long-View has the highest peak around.
Somehow I'd never climbed its cragged heights,

its rocky cliffs like walls hacked and scraped
and towering over mountains crowded near,

but today, skies so bright and clear, I set out.
Soon the far end of sight's all boundless away,

Cloud-Dream southlands a trifle in the palm,
Warrior Knoll lost in that realm of blossoms.

And back on my horse, riding home at dusk,
a vine-sifted moon keeps the stream lit deep.

translated from Chinese by
DAVID HINTON

Martwe morze

marzec 1999

Nabrzeże pełne mówiących ryb, sól.
Wyspa jest, broni się resztką pieniędzy,
trochę dryfuje. Inny jest język wyspy,
kiedy rankiem wyłania się z dna, inny

Wieczorem, kiedy przypływ. Prądy i wiry
w łóżku, w kuchni resztki rozbitych statków,
kubki, dzbanek z kawą. Ścięte morze.
Rozbitkowie wypluci przez muł dają sobie

znaki, w ciemności prawa poznają, budują
szałasy, mają dziecko, gotują wodę.
W czajniku sztorm, w łazience ślady stóp
i twarz w ręczniku. Bez flag, sygnałów,

bez map, na dnie miasta. Za wszystkimi
siedmioma drzwiami morze.

TOMASZ RÓŻYCKI

The Dead Sea

March 1999

The quay is full of talking fish; salt.
There is an island, it defends itself with the money that's left,
It drifts a little. It has different languages—one
When it breaks the surface in the morning, and one

For the evening tide. Currents swirl
In bed, shattered vessels in the kitchen,
Cups, a jug of coffee. The sea is coagulated.
The castaways, spat out by slime, sign

To each other, learn the laws in the dark, build
Shacks, have children, boil the water.
There's a storm in the kettle, footprints in the bathroom
A face on the towel. No flags, signals,

No maps at the bottom of the city. The sea
Behind all seven doors.

translated from Polish by
JACEK GUTOROW

La Demande

Tu travailles pour le fric ou pour
La baise? demande à l'infirmière
Une femme que les policiers amènent
Prise dans une colère qui n'est déjà
Plus à elle. Elle crie: *Les poules*
Du haut finissent toujours par salir
Celles d'en bas, et s'en va
Vers le lit bancal où la chère
Innocence se fait une fois encore
Recoudre le pucelage. *Vous ne voulez*
Jamais sauver, ajoute-t-elle,
Que ce qui est perdu.
                              La télévision,
Ecrit l'interne sur le formulaire,
Semble avoir cessé de l'intéresser.

HÉDI KADDOUR

The Question

Do you work for the dough or to
Get laid? the nurse is asked by
A woman who's brought in by the police
Seized by a rage that is no longer
Entirely hers. She shouts *The hens*
On top always end up shitting
On the ones below, and goes off towards
The rickety bed where her dear
Innocence will have its hymen
Mended once more. *You never*
Want to save anything, she adds,
But what's already lost.
                    Television,
Writes the intern on her chart,
Seems to have stopped interesting her.

translated from French by
MARILYN HACKER

Déesse de Printemps

À Jean-Pierre Lemaire

Le temps s'est efface où defense
Est faite de manger du lièvre,
De crainte de que ne se transmît
À l'homme la lubricité de cet animal
Nocturne et sodomite qui boxe
Sa compagne avant de la monter.
Les enfants ce matin cherchent
Du chocolat dans l'herbe fraîche,
Et l'Église en verve fait retentir
Les cloches d'une Résurrectipn
Tandis qu'un homme à la recherché
De pieces d'or met au jour les os
Rompus et calcinés d'une prêtresse
D'*Oster*, déesse aux grandes hases.

HÉDI KADDOUR

Goddess of Spring

for Jean-Pierre Lemaire

Erased from our annals is the time when
It was forbidden to eat hare for fear
That humans might be infected
With the lechery of that nocturnal
Sodomite of an animal who boxes
With his mate before mounting her.
This morning children are out hunting
For chocolate in the damp grass
And the church, in top form, sounds out
The bells of a Resurrection
While a man searching for gold
Coins unearths the calcinated bone
Shards of a priestess of *Oster*,
Goddess flanked by giant she-hares.

translated from French by
MARILYN HACKER

La Librairie du Scarabée

Comme sur le perron d'un rêve
La jupe rose un noeud dans les chrveux,
À soixante ans, *"t'as pas cent balles"*
Réclame-t-elle à celui qui regarde
Sa jeunesse dans les livres anciens,
Le voyage de Babar, Mticho
L'ourson sans mere dans la vitrine,
Avec derrière l'épaule les vieux
Amours venus rôder au bord
De la montagne Sainte-Geneviève.
Temps où on s'est laissé glisser
Sur son ombre tandis qu'au reflux
De la mémoire monte en sublime
Odeur un rot d'alcool pas cher.

HÉDI KADDOUR

The Scarab Bookshop

It might be on the front steps of a dream,
Her pink skirt, the ribbon in her hair
At sixty. "Can you spare me a tenner?"
She insists, as you stare
At your own childhood in those old books
Babar's Journey, Mitchi
The Bearcub, motherless in the window
While, behind your back, all of your old
Loves have returned to lurk around
The foot of the Montagne Ste-Geneviève.
A time when you have let yourself slip
On your own shadow, while on memory's
Ebb-tide there rises in sublime
Odiferousness, a belch of cheap booze.

translated from French by
MARILYN HACKER

Enseña a morir antes y que la mayor parte de la muerte es la vida, y ésta no se siente, y la menor, que es el último suspiro, es la que da pena

Señor don Juan, pues con la fiebre apenas
se calienta la sangre desmayada,
y por la mucha edad, desabrigada,
tiembla, no pulsa, entre la arteria y venas;

pues que de nieve están las cumbres llenas,
la boca, de los años saqueada,
la vista, enferma, en noche sepultada,
y las potencias, de ejercicio ajenas,

salid a recibir la sepoltura,
acariciad la tumba y monumento:
que morir vivo es última cordura.

La mayor parte de la muerte siento
que se pasa en contentos y locura,
y a la menor se guarda el sentimiento.

FRANCISCO DE QUEVEDO

He Teaches How to Die Beforehand and That the Greater Part of Death Is Life, and This You Don't Feel, and the Lesser, Which Is the Last Breath, Is That Which Causes Pain

Señor don Juan, since taken with fever
it barely heats up, your disgruntled blood,
and much of the time, stripped to the core,
it shivers without pulse between artery and veins

Since the clouds have grown full of snow
your mouth, from many years grown shaky
your sight, sickly, buried in perpetual night
and your virility a hopeless game

go gladly accept the weight of your burial
hold tenderness for the tomb and headstone
"I live in order to die" is the ultimate proverb

The greater part of death comes over me
in moments of insanity and contentment
and the lesser when I gain over emotions control.

translated from Spanish by
PAMELA GREENBERG

敬亭獨坐

眾鳥高飛盡
孤雲去獨閒
相看兩不厭
唯有敬亭山

山中與幽人對酌

兩人對酌山花開
一盃一盃復一盃
我醉欲眠卿且去
明朝有意抱琴來

LI PO

Two Too Free Translations of Poems by Li Po

Sitting Alone at Ching-t'ing Peak

gabble,gaggle, the birds flown off
one white cloud just sits here
one white haired me just sits here too
then just One
of us, All.

Drinking in the Mountains with a Hermit Friend

You and me and a bottle:
mountain flowers, opening.
A shot, a shot, another
shot. Damn am I drunk; *you* can go now.
If you please, in the morning,
you can come back. Bring your guitar.

translated from Chinese by
J. P. SEATON

Mstivá kantiléna

I

Oh moje Manon! To juž není nesmělý Váš abbé,
jenž k sličné Manon chodil, stonavé a nudou slabé,

a při němž Manon doufávala: snad se dneska vzmuží
a začne slibovanou legendu o hříchu žlutých růží...

Oh moje Manon! Zvykejte! Dnes hlas mám příliš tvrdý
a jako Geus jen na svůj hlad si mohu býti hrdý.

Já schvalně opustil své soudruhy a rodná pole,
bych zazpívat Vám mohl kantilénu při viole,

a mstivou kantilénu, v níž by moje ústa chabá
Vám vyčtla, že jste spíše hladem nežli nudou slabá,

a v níž by vzmužily se moje oči bez tepla
nad legendou, jak luna dlouhým pláčem oslepla...

Vím, že má Manon všecka nervózní je z všeho toho,
že ráda by si lhala starou touhu pro někoho,

a zatím ticho trapné, ticho rozespalé všady
na uvítanou *jinému* se snáší nad zahrady.

III

To bylo lstivé kyrie, jež navečer vsí pustou lkalo,
za naše pole, které dlouhou bázní neplodné se stalo—
to byla prosba za teplo, jež hlas náš, mdlý a nevyspalý,
pro naše ženy chtěl, jež dlouhou bázní neplodné se staly.

To bylo lstivé kyrie za naše mladé ženy lysé,
my za ně denně prosili a štkali, ve tmách plazili se,
my bez reptání každým hladem pro ně mřeli ve svém žití—
však tímto hladem, Pane, tímto hladem nechtěli jsme mříti!

(continued)

A Vengeful Cantilena

I

O my Manon! I'll no longer play the craven, white-livered abbé,
who to dear, sickly Manon used to go—and next to whom

Manon, weak with spleen, slyly hoped: "Today, perhaps, he'll be bold
and at last begin the Legend of the Yellow Roses' Sin..."

O my Manon! Get used to it! Today, my voice is cruel,
and, like a Gueux, only my servile hunger fuels my pride.

Resolutely, I left my comrades and my native fields
to sing to you a cantilena to the trills of my viola—

A vengeful cantilena, with which my anemic mouth
reviles you: From starvation, not from boredom, you are weak—

And at which my death-like eyes spark,
retelling the Legend of How the Moon Went Blind from Long Weeping...

I know that my Manon is all nervous about this—
that clearly she would rather lie to herself an old desire for someone else—

And meanwhile, a shameless silence, sleepy-eyed and shrewd,
in welcome of *Another* descends over the gardens...

III

It was a wily kyrie, wailed at evening through the deserted hamlet,
a kyrie for our fields, which, through long terror, had grown infertile—
it was a plea for warmth, which our voices, anemic and strained,
begged for our women, who, through long terror, had grown infertile.

It was a wily kyrie for our bald young women—
daily, we pleaded on their behalf, sobbing, we groveled in darkness,
and, without protest, we died of every last hunger for them—
but of *this* hunger, O God, of *this* hunger we did not care to die!

(continued)

A když pak ve vášnivém náručí nám opět umíraly
i ženy poslední, jež dlouhou bázní neplodné se staly,
my se zaťatou, mstivou pěstí, se zaťatým mstivým hledem
jsme smýkali tvým jménem, divoce ho ve tmách řvali:

že zrovna tuhle vášeň—slyšíš? slyšíš?—v našem těle snědém
my udusit a na oltář ti hodit nikdy nedovedem!

IV

Zas den byl ospalý—po proudu řeky kdosi šel—
pod smutným nebem, nebem nízkým, nebem bez tepla—
to den byl ospalý—kdos zádumčivě v dálce pěl:
že marno vše, že nevzroste nic, že nic nevzeplá.

A večer sychravý byl, zimomřivá nálada,
a všady bázlivě si lehli, světla zhasili,
když náhle vzpomněli, že marno myslet na lada,
že ani letos nevzejde, co před léty tam zasili.

Noc byla zamlklá—kdos podle řeky ještě šel—
byl měsíc v mracích, v mracích smutných, měsíc bez tepla,
na břehu protějším kdos zádumčivou píseň pěl:
Že marno vše.—Že nevzroste nic.—Že nic nevzeplá.

IX

Byl deštivý soumrak—a vítr se za řekou bál,
a světla se bála, a báli se nemocní psi,
již bojácně štěkali chvílemi z rozmoklých skal,
oh—báli se odvčera, báli se do prázdných vsí.

Ač včera již navečer hnali je důtkami z bud,
než odešli za řeku, vítr kde bojácně pěl,
psi nemocní štěkali, štěkali z rozmoklých hrud,
a hlas jejich vychrtlý chvílemi zimou se chvěl.

Neb v chalupách při lampě zkoušeli broušenou zbraň,
a k půlnoci teprv, když běhoun se vesnicí hnal
a smluvené heslo dal: Staniž se—staniž se—staň!,
psy nemocné za klení hnali až do rodných skal—
a sami se srotili, sami na rozmoklou pláň.

(continued)

And later, when they were dying in our crazed embrace—
the last of the women, who, through long terror, had grown infertile—
we looted your name, we defiled it with our fists in the blackness, shouting:

this craving—Do you hear?—This craving in our sinewy bodies
we will never choke out and throw upon your altar!

IV

Again the day was sleepy—Someone was walking down the river—
under a funereal sky, a sunken sky, a sky without warmth—
the day was sleepy—Someone sang bleakly in the distance:
that all is in vain, that nothing will grow, nothing will burst into flame.

And bone-chilling, the evening—A hypothermic mood,
and everywhere, terrified, they lay in their beds, lights extinguished,
when suddenly they remembered that it was vain to think of the shriveled fields—
that what was sown years ago wouldn't sprout this year either.

The night was silent—Still someone kept walking down the river—
the rueful moon, moon without warmth, fled into the clouds,
and on the opposite shore, someone sang bleakly:
All is in vain—Nothing will ever grow—Nothing will burst into flame.

IX

It was a rainy nightfall—On the other side of the river, the wind sang out, afraid,
and the lights, too, stood afraid, and afraid, the sickly dogs,
who, from time to time, barked form the soaking rocks, afraid,
o—afraid, after yesterday, to go into the deserted villages.

Yesterday, at evening, they'd driven the dogs out of their pens
before they left to cross the river, to where the wind sang out, afraid—
and the sickly dogs barked, they barked from the soaking soil,
their thin voices, from time to time, trembling with cold.

By lantern-light, yesterday, they'd tested whetted blades,
and only near midnight, when a lone messenger dashed into the village
and gave the secret password—*Let it be now!—Let it be now!*—
did they drive out the sickly dogs, with blaspheming and cursing, to their native rocks

and they themselves formed a riotous mob out on the soaking plain.

(continued)

X

Snad na sta jich sedělo uprostřed náměstí kol prázdných stolů
(byl slavnostní večer a jejich bůh zažehal po nebi síru)
a zraky jich s oblohy šilhaly pokradmu k radnici dolů...
oh, v městě si chytili biskupa, pro jeho zuřivou víru.

Oh, chytili tlustého biskupa, jídával boha prý svého
a posílal proti nim lancknechty, posměšně tupil jich víru—
dnes slavnostní chystají večer si z biskupa, z biskupa ctného,
a jejich bůh k hodu jim zažehá po nebi dusivou síru.

Tak strnule seděli hladoví uprostřed náměstí spolu
a zraky jich dychtivě šilhaly k radnici od prázdných stolů.

KAREL HLAVÁČEK

X

About a hundred of them sat in the square, sat around the empty tables
(it was a festive evening, their god was flashing sulfur down from the heavens)
and their eyes crept stealthily to the town hall below...
o in the city, they'd caught themselves a bishop renowned for his furious faith.

O they caught themselves a fat bishop, who used to eat his god,
who sent mercenaries against them, who mockingly vilified their faith,
and now they're making a festive evening out of the bishop, the virtuous bishop,
and, for the feast, their god is igniting choking sulfur across the heavens.

So stiffly they sat, starving in the middle of the square,
and their eyes crept greedily from the empty tables down to the town hall.

translated from Czech by
JOSEF HORÁČEK & LARA GLENUM

Vaca negra sobre fundo rosa

Até os cinco anos de idade jamais havia visto um trem de carga;
e até os oito anos jamais um meteorologista
                              A garota com sombrinha chinesa
foi um dia a minha garota com sombrinha chinesa, e a este
que brinca na areia da praia chamamos nosso filho, pois
é o que é, como a bola azul em suas mãos é a bola azul
em suas mãos e o verão é outra bola azul em suas mãos.
As coisas são o que são e sei que antes de precisar
outra vez barbear-me já terão voltado para o frio
de seu novo país. E talvez em meus sonhos
voltem a fazer falta as três dimensões
desse mundo espesso como uma
vaca negra sobre fundo rosa.

CARLITO AZEVEDO

Black cow on a pink ground

Until I was five I had never seen a freight train;
until eight, a meteorologist.
                    The girl with a Chinese umbrella
was once my girl with a Chinese umbrella, and this
one who plays on the beach we call our son, since
things are like that, the way the blue ball in his hands is the blue ball
in his hands and summer another blue ball in his hands.
Things are what they are, and I know that before I need to shave
again they will have already returned to the cold
of their new country. And perhaps in my dreams
the three dimensions will be missing again
from a world as thick as a
black cow on a pink ground.

translated from Portuguese by
FLÁVIA ROCHA

Do Livro das Viagens

Liliana Ponce não esqueceu seu casaco no salão de chá
Liliana Ponce nem estava de casaco
(No Rio de Janeiro fazia um belíssimo dia de sol e dava gosto olhar cada ferida
    exposta na pedra)
Liliana Ponce, conseqüentemente, não teve que voltar às pressas para a casa de chá
(a garçonete com cara de flautista da Sinfônica de São Petersburgo não veio nos
    alcançar à saída ascenando um casaco esquecido)
Desse modo Liliana Ponce chegou a tempo de pegar o avião
Partiu para a Argentina

CARLITO AZEVEDO

The Book of Travel

Liliana Ponce didn't forget her coat in the tea-room
Liliana Ponce didn't even wear a coat
(In Rio de Janeiro it was a beautiful sunny day and a pleasure to look at each wound
exposed in stone)
Consequently, Liliana Ponce didn't have to rush back to the tea-room
(The waitress with a face of a Saint Petersburg Orchestra flutist didn't catch up with
us at the exit waving a forgotten coat)
For Liliana Ponce arrived in time to take the plane
She left for Argentina

translated from Portuguese by
FLÁVIA ROCHA

Irla

Igandea da hondartzan asmo oneko jendearentzat.
Hango harrabots urruna entzuten da irlatik.

Uretara sartu gara biluzik,
Anemonak, trikuak, barbarinak ikusi ditugu hondoan.
Begira, haizeak garia bezala mugitzen du urak hondarra.
Urpera sartu eta azpitik begiratu zaitut.
Atsegin dut esku eta zangoen mugimendu geldoa,
Atsegin sabelpeak itsasbelarren forma hartzean.

Lehorrera igo gara. Bero da eta itzal egiten dute pinuek.
Gaziak dira zure besoak, gazia bularra, sabela gazia.
Ilargia itsasoarekin lotzen duen indar berak
lotu gaitu geu ere.
Mendeak segundo bihurtu dira eta segundoak mende.
Udare zurituak gure gorputzak.

Anemonak, trikuak, barbarinak ikusi ditugu hondoan.
Igandea da hondartzan asmo oneko jendearentzat.

KIRMEN URIBE

72

The Island

It's Sunday on the beach for all people of good desires.
You can hear the faraway noise of it from the island.

We go into the water naked,
We see anemones, red mullets, sea-thistles on the bayfloor.
Look—like the wind the wheat the water moves the sand.
I go under and behold you from underneath.
I like the slow movement of your hands and legs.
I like your underbelly's taking the form of seaweed.

We go up on dry land. It's hot and the pines make shadow.
Your arms are salty, your chest salty, belly salty.
The same power that joins the moon with the sea
has joined us too.
Centuries become a second and seconds centuries.
Our bodies, peeled pears.

We see anemones, red mullets, sea-thistles on the bayfloor.
It's Sunday on the beach for all people of good desires.

translated from Basque by
ELIZABETH MACKLIN

Ezin Esan

Ezin da esan Libertatea, ezin da esan Berdintasuna,
ezin da esan Anaitasuna, ezin esan.
Ez zuhaitz ez erreka ez bihotz.
Ahaztu egin da antzinako legea.

Uholak eraman du hitzen eta gauzen arteko zubia.
Ezin zaio esan tiranoak erabaki irizten dionari heriotza.
Ezin da esan norbait falta dugunean,
oroitzapen txikienak odolusten gaituenean.

Inperfektua da hizkuntza, higatu egin dira zeinuak
errotarri zaharrak bezala, ibiliaren ibiliz. Horregatik,

ezin da esan Maitasuna, ezin da esan Edertasuna,
ezin da esan Elkartasuna, ezin esan.
Ez zuhaitz ez erreka ez bihotz.
Ahaztu egin da antzinako legea.

Alabaina "ene maitea" zure ahotik entzutean
aitor dut zirrara eragiten didala,
dela egia, dela gezurra.

KIRMEN URIBE

No Saying

No saying Liberty, no saying Equality,
no saying Fraternity—can't say it.
Not tree not stream not heart.
The ancienter law is been forgot.

The flood's taken out the bridge from words to things.
Can't call what a tyrant thinks to decide death.
No saying when we're longing for somebody's presence,
when the smallest reminder empties the blood from a vein.

The language is unperfected, the signs worn down
as old millstones—the action of action. That's how come

no saying Love, no saying Beauty,
no saying Solidarity—can't say it.
Not tree not stream not heart.
The ancienter law is been forgot.

Though when I've heard "My love" from your mouth,
I confess it has thrilled my being—
Whether it's true or if a lie.

translated from Basque by
ELIZABETH MACKLIN

De Profundis

Es ist ein Stoppelfeld, in das ein schwarzer Regen fällt.
Es ist ein brauner Baum, der einsam dasteht.
Es ist ein Zischelwind, der leere Hütten umkreist.
Wie traurig dieser Abend.

Am Weiler vorbei
Sammelt die sanfte Waise noch spärliche Ähren ein.
Ihre Augen weiden rund und goldig in der Dämmerung
Und ihr Schoß harrt des himmlischen Bräutigams.

Bei der Heimkehr
Fanden die Hirten den süßen Leib
Verwest im Dornenbusch.

Ein Schatten bin ich ferne finsteren Dörfern.
Gottes Schweigen
Trank ich aus dem Brunnen des Hains.

Auf meine Stirne tritt kaltes Metall
Spinnen suchen mein Herz.
Est ist ein Licht, das in meinem Mund erlöscht.

Nachts fand ich mich auf einer Heide,
Starrend von Unrat und Staub der Sterne.
Im Haselgebüsch
Klangen wieder kristallne Engel.

GEORG TRAKL

De Profundis

It's a stubble field, where black rain falls.
It's a brown tree, standing all alone.
It's a hissing wind, haunting empty houses—
What a dismal night.

Out past the village
The little orphan gathers corn. She can't find much.
Her sweet round eyes graze, in the twilight,
And her womb hungers for a heavenly husband.

Coming home
The shepherds find her dear body
Rotting in the brambles.

I am a shadow, far from miserable villages.
I drank God's silence
From the forest streams.

The cold metal comes clear on my forehead.
Spiders hunt for my heart.
It's a light, dying in my mouth.

At night I found myself on a moor,
Numbed, frozen by shit and by dust from the stars.
In the hazel bush
Crystal angels have been rising again.

translated from German by
BURTON RAFFEL

Klage

Schlaf und Tod, die düstern Adler
Umrauschen nachtlang dieses Haupt:
Des Menschen goldnes Bildnis
Verschlänge die eisige Woge
Der Ewigkeit. An schaurigen Riffen
Zerschellt der purpurne Leib
Und es klagt die dunkle Stimme
Über dem Meer.
Schwester stürmischer Schwermut
Sieh ein ängstlicher Kahn versinkt
Unter Sternen,
Dem schweigenden Antlitz der Nacht.

GEORG TRAKL

Lament

Two gloomy eagles, Sleep and Death,
Circle soft around and around
This head, circle all night long:
Man's golden ikon dropping into
Eternity's cold waves. Red flesh
Ripped on vicious reefs.
And a dark voice weeping
Across the sea.
Sister of wild sadness,
See a frightened little boat
Sink under the stars, under
Night's portentous dumb face.

translated from German by
BURTON RAFFEL

An Obair

An móta is bábhún Normannach a chonac isteach thar chuirtín crann
is mé ag tiomáint thar bráid go tapaidh at an mbóthar,
áit éigin faoin dtuath in aice le Cill Mhaighneann
i cgCo. na Mí, a thugann an ainm don áit. Sin í An Obair.

É sin is an cara mná is ansa loim ar domhan ag fáil bháis go mall
in Ospidéal an Adelaide: an grianghraf thíos im' phóca dúinn beirt inár mná óga
a tógadh lá Márta, an chéad lá earraigh i nGairdín na mBláth in Ankara
na Tuirce: sinn ag gáirí is gan tuairim againn ar cad a bhí romhainn:

aghaidh na mná Moslamaí ón Ailgéir a chonac le déanaí sa nuachtán
nuair a hinsíodh di go rabhthas tar éis an scornach a ghearradh
ar ochtar leanbh óg dá clann: an file iomráiteach Seirbeach
a bhí ina cheannaire ar mhórchampa géibhinn; an stairí litríochta
a chaith a chuid ama saor lena chairde ag imirt caide le plaosc dhaonna:

m'fhear céile a chaith sé lá i gcóma is mé ag féachaint amach fuinneoga
an tseomra feithimh ar an solas ag dorchú amuigh ar an mbá
idir Dún Laoghaire is Beann Éadair, is ar theacht is imeacht na taoide:
trácht trom ar an mbóthar mar a raibh an saol Fódlach ag rith sall
is anall, ag plódú ar nós na nduilleog a bhí ag péacadh ar gach aon chrann:

—é sea go léir a thabhairt faoi ndeara is áit a dhéanamh dó id' chroí gan pléascadh,
é seo uile is an móta Normannach a chonac is mé ag gabháil na slí,
áit éigin faoin dtuath in aice le Cill Mhaighneann i gCo. na Mí—
An Obair. Sin í an obair. Sin í an obair nach éasca.

NUALA NÍ DHOMNHAILL

The Task

It's from the massive Norman earthworks I glimpsed through a curtain of trees
as I drove quickly past,
somewhere near Kilmainham, County Meath,
that the place took its name. Nobber. From the Irish *an obair*, "the task".

From that and my dearest friend slowly dying
in the Adelaide Hospital; the photograph deep in my pocket of us as young women,
taken on a March day, the first day of spring in the Botanic Gardens in Ankara,
laughing, with no sense of what was to come;

the face of the Muslim woman from Algeria I saw in a newspaper lately
after she was told lately that the throats
of eight of her children had been cut; the major Serbian poet
who was the commandant of a major camp; the literary historian
who enjoyed an off-moment with his friends, playing ball with a human skull;

my own husband who spent six days in a coma while I looked out the windows
of the waiting room at the light going down on the bay
between Dun Laoghaire and Howth, at the come and go of the tide;
heavy traffic on the road as the entire population of Ireland rushed here and there,
countless as bud-blasts from the trees;

to take it all in, to make room in your heart without having your heart burst,
to take in not only this but the Norman motte and bailey
I passed near Kilmainham or thereabouts,
a place called Nobber. That's the task. *An obair.* A task that's far from easy.

translated from Irish by
PAUL MULDOON

Oda Con un Lamento

Oh niña entre las rosas, oh presión de palomas,
oh presidio de peces y rosales,
tu alma es una botella llena de sal sedienta
y una campana llena de uvas es tu piel.

Por desgracia no tengo para darte sino uñas
o pestañas, o pianos derretidos,
o sueños que salen de mi corazón a borbotones,
polvorientos sueños que corren como jinetes negros,
sueños llenos de velocidades y desgracias.

Sólo puedo quererte con besos y amapolas,
con guirnaldas mojadas por la lluvia,
mirando cenicientos caballos y perros amarillos.
Sólo puedo quererte con olas a la espalda,
entre vagos golpes de azufre y agues ensimismadas,
nadando en contra de los cementerios que corren en ciertos ríos
con pasto mojado creciendo sobre las tristes tumbas de veso
nadando a través de corazones sumergidos
y pálidas planillas de niños insepultos.

Hay mucha muerte, muchos acontecimientos funerarios
en mis desamparadas pasiones y desolados besos,
hay el agua que cae en mi cabeza,
mientras crece mi pelo,
un agua como el tiempo, un agua negra desencadenada,
con una voz nocturna, con un grito
de pájaro en la lluvia, con una interminable
sombra de ala mojada que protege mis huesos:
mientras me visto, mientras
interminablemente me miro en los espejos y en los vidrios,
oigo que alguien me sigue llamándome a sollozos
con una triste voz podrida por el tiempo.

Tú estás de pie sobre la tierra, llena
de dientes y relámpagos.
Tú propagas los besos y matas las hormigas.
Tú lloras de salud, de cebolla, de abeja,
de abecedario ardiendo.
Tú eres como una espada azul y verde
y ondulas al tocarte, como un río.

(continued)

Ode with a Lament

Oh girl among roses, oh pressure of doves,
oh garrison of fish and rosebushes,
your soul is a bottle full of thirsty salt
and a bell full of grapes is your skin.

I have nothing, alas, to give you but fingernails
or eyelashes or molten pianos,
or dreams frothing from my heart,
dust dreams racing like black horsemen,
dreams full of velocity and misfortune.

Looking at ash-colored horses and yellow dogs,
I can only love you with poppies and kisses,
with garlands drenched by the rain.
I can only love you with waves at my shoulder,
between vague blows of sulpher and brooding water,
swimming against the cemeteries flowing down certain rivers,
wet fodder growing over the sad plaster tombs,
swimming across submerged hearts
and the pallid birth certificates of dug-up children.

There is so much death, so many funerals
in my abandoned passions, my desolate kisses,
there is a water falling on my head,
while my hair grows,
a water like time, a liberated black water
with a nocturnal voice, with a cry
of birds in the rain, with an interminable
shadow of damp wings protecting my bones:
while I dress, while
interminably I stare at mirrors, at windowpanes,
I hear someone pursue me calling me
sobbing in a voice rotted by time.

You are standing on the earth, full
of lightning and teeth.
You spread kisses and murder ants.
You weep from health, from onions, from bees,
from a burning alphabet.
You are like a blue and green sword
and undulate to my touch like a river.   *(continued)*

83

Ven a mi alma vestida de blanco, con un ramo
de ensangrentadas rosas y copas de cenizas,
ven con una manzana y un caballo,
porque allí hay una sala oscura y un candelabro roto,
unas sillas torcidas que esperan el invierno,
y una paloma muerta, con un número.

PABLO NERUDA

Come to my soul dressed in white, with a branch
of blood-smeared roses, and goblets of ashes,
come with an apple and a horse—
for here there is a dark parlour, a broken candelabrum,
some warped chairs waiting for winter,
and a pigeon dead, with a number.

translated from Spanish by
CLAYTON ESHLEMAN

ο]ἰ μὲν ἰππήων στρότον οἰ δὲ πέσδων
οἰ δὲ νάων φαῖσ’ ἐπ[ὶ] γᾶν μέλαι[ν]αν
ἔ]μμεναι κάλλιστον, ἔγω δὲ κῆν’ ὅτ-
τω τις ἔραται·

πά]γχυ δ’ εὔμαρες σύνετον πόησαι
π]άντι τ[ο]ῦτ’, ἀ γὰρ πόλυ περσκέθοισα
κάλλος [ἀνθ]ρώπων Ἐλένα [τὸ]ν ἄνδρα
τὸν [πανάρ]ιστον

καλλ[ίποι]σ’ ἔβα ’ς Τροΐαν πλέοι [σα
κωὐδ[ὲ πα]ῖδος οὐδὲ φίλων το[κ]ήων
πά[μπαν] ἐμνάσθη, ἀλλὰ παράγαγ’ αὔταν
          ]σαν

          ]αμπτον γὰρ]
       ]. . . κούφως τ[   ]οησ[.]ν
. .]με νῦν Ἀνακτορί[ας ὀ]νέμναι-
σ’ οὐ] παρεοίσας·

τᾶ]ς κε βολλοίμαν ἔρατόν τε βᾶμα
κἀμάρυχμα λάμπρον ἴδην προσώπω
ἢ τὰ Λύδων ἄρματα κἀν ὄπλοισι
πεσδομ]άχεντας.

          ]. μεν οὐ δύνατον γένεσθαι
          ]. ν ἄνθρωπ[. . . π]εδέχην δ’ ἄρασθαι

τ’ ἐξ ἀδοκή[τω.

After Sappho, Fragments
Fragment 16

Some say a host of horsemen, a horizon of ships
under sail is most beautiful but I say it is whatever
you love I say it is
you

        neither the women of the city rising
          over the lake nor those of the
            medieval towns
        shining on the riverred island nor
     the beauties floating down these gridded
        taxi'd streets nor any
           man ever
         is pleasing to my
           eyes but
            you

Fragment 16

I would rather see your face
than all . . . .

```
                    ] ω [
               ] ϲαν ἐν τῶι . [
          ] . δὲ ῖ κ(αὶ) ἑκάστης ὁ ᾶ[

     ] . εν τὸ γὰρ ἐννεπε[ . ]η προβ[
     ] . ατε τὰν εὔποδα νύμφαν  [
     ]τα παῖδα Κρονίδα τὰν ἰόκ[ολπ]ον[
     ] . ϛ ὄργαν θεμένα τὰν ἰόκ[ολ]πος α[
        ] . . ἄγναι Χάριτες Πιέριδέ [ϛ τε] Μοῖ[σαι
          ] . [ . ὄ]ππποτ' ἀοιδαι φρέν[ . . . ]αν . [
               ]ϲαιοισα λιγύραν [ἀοί]δαν
               γά]μβρον, ἄσαροι γὰρ ὐμαλικ[
                  ]σε φόβαισι θεμέγα λύρα . [
               ] . . η χρυσοπέδιλ‹λ› [ο]ϛ Αὔως
```

SAPPHO

90

Fragment 103

It's true the charm may lie
                    somewhat
        in the subject such as gardens
                            wedding songs love affairs
        against these few will speak and all
                            at one time
                may have hoped—
        but there is your bending
                neck and the small hollow at the base
                    of your long back
                    and no charm
                    other

        song likes its own delights and even sadness
                in some modes
                        charms
                those whose hearts have moved
                    so

        what to do with the soul
                        its many
                            motions

                            translated from Ancient Greek by
                            MAUREEN N. McLANE

Fidélité

Non, je n'ai point fêlé mon vase d'or.
Tes yeux font délirer toujours comme un vin de palme nouveau.
La terre n'a rien bu de mon amour.
Sur les roniers, sentinelles à l'aube,
Ramiers et tourterelles
Roucoulent l'appel aux libations quotidiennes.
Les jours ont avalé les nuits,
Les saisons sèches ont bu Niger et Gambie,
Des hordes de baisers farouches
Assiègent depuis longtemps ma puissante Tombouctou.
Mais ton parfum, qui reste frais, brise
Pour moi seul son flacon au lever.
Et dans l'ivresse, je sacrifie
Après l'ablution à la fontaine claire.

LÉOPOLD SÉDAR SENGHOR

from Oeuvre poétique © Editions du Seuil, 1990

Fidelity

No, I did not
crack my golden vase.
Your eyes always create
delirium like a new palm wine.
The earth has drunk
nothing of my love.
On the palmyra trees,
wood pigeons and turtledoves
sentries at dawn
coo the call to daily libations.
Days have devoured nights,
dry seasons have drunk the Niger and Gambia,
hordes of fierce kisses have
besieged my indomitable Timbuktu.
But your ever-fresh perfume
breaks its raised flask for me alone.
In the drunkenness
I sacrifice
after ablutions at the clear spring.

translated from French by
KRISTEN ANDERSEN

The Wall Street Inferno

Written in New York in the 1870s, Canto X of the monumental verse epic *O Guesa errante (Wandering Guesa)* by the Brazilian poet Joaquim Maria de Sousândrade (1833-1902), an episode also known as "The Wall Street Inferno," presents a Dantesque vision of the Gilded Age of American capitalism. Before his 14-year New York sojourn, Sousândrade, a native of Maranhão (Northeastern Brazil), had studied in Paris and traveled widely in France, Portugal, and England. Like Gonçalves Dias, a fellow exiled Romantic poet from the previous generation, Sousândrade too addressed the question of national affirmation in his poetry, thus establishing a dialogue with European Romanticism. At the time, Brazil's quest for independence fueled a reaction against the Portuguese metropolis, resulting in a political transition from a monarchy to republic. The search for development models suitable for a country in the throes of modernization led Brazilians to consider, among other things, the American political and economic system, which Sousândrade came to know first-hand and critically portrayed in the "Wall Street" episode of his *Guesa*.

The entire epic, a 350+-page poem partly inspired by Humboldt's travel writings, charts the trans-American wanderings of *Guesa* ("the errant one"), a mythological figure in the tradition of the Muisca Indians of Nueva Granada (Colombia). According to Muisca belief, Guesa, a young boy, is taken away from the custody of his parents and raised until age ten in the temple dedicated to Bochica, a sun divinity. From that age until 15, he roams the continent touring all the locations visited by Bochica, before being taken to his final destination, to be ritually sacrificed by the sun priests or *xeques*.

"The Wall Street Inferno" opens as Guesa, believing he has escaped death at the hands of the xeques, finds himself descending into the nightmarish turmoil of the New York Stock Exchange. There, in a sequence that also reminds us of Goethe's Faustian Walpurgisnacht episodes, Guesa bears witness to an anarchically carnivalesque parade of events and characters—historical, contemporary, literary, and mythological. These bizarre juxtapositions were meant to denounce the contradictions of turn-of-the-century capitalism, epitomized by financial, social, and political scandals. Sousândrade's modern-day "Inferno" is an enigmatic "montage of news items from the papers of his time . . . a chaotic, polyglot whirl," to quote the Brazilian poet Haroldo de Campos (1929–2003), who along with his brother and fellow poet, Augusto de Campos, rescued Sousândrade's bold, original work from oblivion, producing, since the mid-1960s, important Brazilian editions of his work.

Among the innovations introduced by Sousândrade and which earn him a place as one of the precursors of Brazilian avant-garde poetry are the use of numerous words in foreign languages and neologisms (such as "free-loves" and "self-help"), highly imaginative rhymes, as well as experimentation with typography, a practice clearly influenced by the massive circulation of illustrated journals at the time. This audacious experimentalism, however, presents a particular challenge to the translator, since it is not always possible to reproduce Sousândrade's peculiar rhymes or intricate wordplay.

To my knowledge, this is the first English translation of selections from "The Wall Street Inferno" to be published in this country. It was carried out in 2000–2001 with the invaluable help and encouragement of the contemporary Brazilian poet Régis Bonvicino, who also aided in the selection of the stanzas translated.

ODILE CISNEROS

d'O Inferno de Wall Street

(O Guesa tendo atravessado as Antilhas, crê-se livre
Xèques e penetra em New-York-Stock-Exchange;
a Voz, *dos desertos:)*

   —Orpheu, Dante, Æneas, ao inferno
Desceram; o Inca ha de subir . . .
       =*Ogni sp'ranza lasciate,*
         Che entrate . . .
   —Swedenborg, ha mundo porvir?

(Xèques surgindo risonhos e disfarçados em Railroad-
managers, Stockjobbers, Pimpbrokers, etc., etc.,
apregoando:)

    —Hárlem! Erie! Central! Pennsylvania!
    =Milhão! cem milhões!! mil milhões!!!
       —Young é Grant! Jackson,
         Atkinson!
Vanderbilts, Jay Goulds, anões!

   (A Voz mal ouvida d'entre a trovoada:)

   —Fulton's *Folly,* Codezo's *Forgery* . . .
Fraude é o clamor da nação!
     Não entendem odes
       Railroads;
Parallela Wall-Street á Chattám . . .

   (Correctores continuando:)

   —Pigmeus, Brown Brothers! Bennett! Steuart!
Rotschild e o ruivalho d'Astor!!
     =Gigantes, escravos
       Se os cravos
Jorram luz, se finda-se a dor! . .

(continued)

from The Wall Street Inferno

(Guesa, having traversed the West Indies, believes himself rid of the Xeques and penetrates the New-York-Stock-Exchange; *the Voice, from the wilderness:*)

—Orpheus, Dante, Aeneas, to hell
Descended; the Inca shall ascend
=*Ogni sp'ranza lasciate,*
Che entrate . . .
—Swedenborg, does fate new worlds portend?

(Smiling Xeques appear disguised as Railroad-*managers,*
Stockjobbers, Pimpbrokers, etc., etc., crying out:)

—Harlem! Erie! Central! Pennsylvania!
=Million! Hundred million!! Billions!! Pelf!!!
—Young is Grant! Jackson,
Atkinson!
Vanderbilts, Jay Goulds like elves!

(The Voice, poorly heard amidst the commotion:)

—Fulton's *Folly,* Codezo's *Forgery . . .*
Fraud cries the nation's bedlam
They grasp no odes
Railroads;
Wall Street's parallel to Chattam . . .

(Brokers going on:)

—Pygmies, Brown Brothers! Bennett! Stewart!
Rothschild and that Astor with red hair!!
=Giants, slaves
If only nails gave
Out streams of light, if they would end despair! . .

(continued)

(Norris, *Attorney*; Codezo, *inventor*; Young, Esq.,
manager; Atkinson, *agent*; Armstrong, *agent*;
Rhodes, *agent*; P. Offman & Voldo, *agents*;
algazarra, miragem; *ao meio, o* Guesa:)

—Dois! três! cinco mil! se jogardes,
Senhor, tereis cinco milhões!
            =Ganhou! ha! haa! haaa!!!
                  —Hurrah! ah!...
      —Sumiram... seriam ladrões?..

(J. Miller nos tectos do *tamanny wigwam* desenrolando
o manto garibaldino:)

—Bloodthirsties! Sioux! ó Modocs!
À White House! Salvai a União,
            Dos Judeus! do exodo
                  Do Godo!
De mais desmoral rebellião!

            *   *   *   *   *

            (*Reporters.*)

—Norris, leis *azues* de Connecticut!
Clevelands, attorney-Cujás,
            Em zebras mudados
                  Forçados,
Dois a dois, aos cem Barrabás!

      (Amigos dos *rêis* perdidos:)

—*Humbug* de *railroad* e telegrapho,
Ao fogo dos céus quiz roubar,
            Que o mundo abrazasse
                  E arvorasse
Por todo elle a *Spangled Star!*

(Um sol rebelde fundando um centro planetar:)

—'George Washington, etc. etc.,
Responda ao Real-George-Tres'!
            =Dizei-lhe, Lord Howe,
                  Real sou...
(E o nariz quebraram do Inglez).

(*continued*)

(NORRIS, *Attorney*; CODEZO, *inventor*; YOUNG, ESQ.,
    manager; ATKINSON, *agent*; ARMSTRONG, *agent*;
    RHODES, *agent*; P. OFFMAN & VOLDO, *agents*;
    hubbub, mirage; in the middle, GUESA:)

—Two! Three! Five thousand! If you play
    Five million, Sir, will you receive
            He won! Hah! Haah!! Haaah!!!
                    —Hurrah! Ah! . . .
    —They vanished . . .   Were they thieves? . .

(J. MILLER atop the roofs of the *Tammany wigwam*
        unfurling the Garibaldian mantle:)

—Bloodthirsties! Sioux! Oh Modocs!
To the White House! Save the Nation,
        From the Jews! From the hazardous
                Goth's Exodus!
From immoral conflagration!

                *   *   *   *   *

            (*Reporters.*)

—Norris, Connecticut's *blue* laws!
Clevelands, attorney-Cujás,
        Into zebras constrained
                Ordained,
Two by two, to one hundred Barabbas!

        (Friends of the lost *kings*:)

—*Humbug* of *railroads* and the telegraph,
The fire of heaven I wished wide and far
        To steal, set the world ablaze
                And above it raise
Forever the *Spangled Star!*

    (A rebellious sun founding a planetary center:)

—'George Washington, etc. etc.,
Answer the Royal-George-Third. Depose!
        =Lord Howe, tell him, do
                I'm royal too . . .
    (And they broke the Englishman's nose).

(continued)

—'Saudar do universo á rainha' . .
Fiança Patriarchas dão sua . . .
(Com rei liberal,
Peor mal,
Fundaram o imperio da lua).

(Reporters:)

—Papel fazem triste na terra
Rêis e poetas, gentes do céu
(E Strauss, o valsando)
Cantando
No Hippodromo ou no Jubileu.

(Correctores achando causa á baixa do câmbio em
WALL-STREET:)

—*Exeunt* Dom Pedro, Dom Grant,
Dom Guesa, que vão navegar:
Seus lemes são de oiro
Que o Moiro
Das vagas amansam do mar.

(Procissão internacional, povo de Israel, Orangianos,
Fenianos, Buddhas, Mormons, Communistas, Nihil-
istas, Farricocos, Railroad-Strikers, All-brockers,
All-jobbers, All-saints, All-devils, lanternas, musica,
sensação; Reporters: passa em LONDON o 'assassino'
da RAINHA e em PARIS 'Lot' o fugitivo de SODOMA:)

—No Espirito-Sancto d'escravos
Ha somente um Imperador;
No dos livres, verso
Reverso,
É tudo coroado Senhor!

(Feiticeiras de KING-ARTHUR e vidente FOSTER em
WALPURGIS de dia:)

—*When the battle's lost and won*—
—*That will be ere the set of sun*—
—*Paddock calls: Anon!*—
—*Fair is foul, and foul is fair:*
Hover through the fog and filthy air!

(continued)

(Satellites greeting JOVE's rays:)

—'Greetings from the universe to the queen' . .
As for bail, the Patriarchs give a boon . . .
(With a liberal king,
A worse thing,
They founded the empire of the moon).

(Reporters:)

—A sorry role on earth they play,
Kings and poets, heaven's aristocracy
(And Strauss, waltzing)
Singing
At the horse races or Jubilee.

(Brokers finding the cause of the WALL STREET market
crash:)

—*Exeunt* Sir Pedro, Sir Grant,
Sir Guesa, seafaring brave:
With gold tillers they endure
The Moor,
Appeased by the turbulent waves.

(International procession, the people of Israel, Orangians,
Fenians, Buddhists, Mormons, Communists, Nihilists,
Penitents, *Railroad-Strikers, All-brokers, All-jobbers,
All-saints, All-devils,* lanterns, music, excitement;
Reporters: in LONDON the QUEEN's 'murderer' passes
by and in PARIS 'Lot' the fugitive from SODOM:)

—In the Holy Spirit of slaves
A single Emperor's renowned
In that of the free, verse
Reverse,
Everything as Lord is crowned!

(KING ARTHUR's witches and clairvoyant FOSTER
on the day of WALPURGIS:)

—*When the battle's lost and won*—
—*That will be ere the set of sun*—
—*Paddock calls: Anon!*—
—*Fair is foul, and foul is fair:*
Hover through the fog and filthy air!

(continued)

(Swedenborg respondendo depois:)

—Ha mundos futuros: república,
Christianismo, céus, Lohengrin.
São mundos presentes:
Patentes,
Vanderbilt-North, Sul-Seraphim.

(Ao fragor de Jerichó encalha Hendrick-Hudson; os Indios vendem aos Hollandezes a ilha de Manhattan *malassombrada:*)

—A Meia-Lua, proa p'ra China,
Está crenando em Tappan-Zee...
Hoogh moghende Heeren...
Pois tirem
Por *guildens* sessenta... *Yea! Yea!*

(*Photophonos-estylographos* direitos sagrados de defeza:)

—Na luz a voz humanitaria:
Odio, não; consciencia e rasão;
Não pornographia;
Isaias
Em biblica vivisecção!

* * * * *

(*Freeloves* passando a votar em seus maridos:)

—De Americanos o unico Emerson,
Não quer prezidencias, o atroz!
═O'bem-justiçados,
Estados
Melhoram p'ra vós e p'ra nós!

(Apocalypticas visões... calumniosas:)

—Pois, 'tendo a Besta patas d' urso,'
In God we trust é o Dragão,
E os falsos-prophetas
Bennettas
Tone, o Theologo e o da Ev'lução!

* * * * *

(continued)

(SWEDENBORG answering later:)

—Future worlds exist: republics,
Christianity, heavens, Lohengrin.
Present worlds are latent:
Patent,
Vanderbilt-North, South-Seraphim.

(At the sound of JERICHO, HENDRICK HUDSON runs
aground; the INDIANS sell the haunted island of
MANHATTAN *to the* DUTCH:)

—The Half-Moon, prow toward China
Is careening in Tappan-Zee...
Hoogh moghende Heeren ...
Take then
For sixty *guilders... Yeah! Yeah!*

(*Photophone-stylographs* sacred right to self-defense:)

—In the light the humanitarian voice:
Not hate; rather conscience, intellection;
Not pornography
Isaiah's prophecy
In Biblical vivisection!

*   *   *   *   *

(*Freeloves* proceeding to vote for their husbands:)

—Among Americans, Emerson alone,
Wants no Presidents, oh atrocious he!
=Oh well-adjudicated,
States
Improve for you, for us, for me!

(APOCALYPTIC visions... slanderous ones:)

—For, 'the Beast having bear's feet,'
In God we trust is the Dragon
And the false prophets
Bennetts
Tone, th' Evolutionist and Theologian!

*   *   *   *   *

(continued)

(Washington 'cegando por causa d'elles'; Pocahontas
sem *personals*:)

—A ursos famintos, cão damnado!
Seja! após festins o festão!. .
    ═Meiga Lulu,
    Choras e tu
Mel ao 'imigo', abelha?. . e ferrão?

(Nariz guatimalo, cornado em facho d'Hymeneu; cora-
ção Dame-Ryder nas envenenadas vidraças do *'too
dark' wedding-pudding*:)

—*'Caramba! yo soy cirurjano*—
Jesuita. . . yankee. . . industrial'!
    —*Job*. . . ou *poisada*,
    Malassombrada,
'Byron' magnetismo-animal!. .

(Practicos mystificadores fazendo seu negócio; *self-help*
Atta-Troll:)

—Que indefeso cáia o extrangeiro,
Que a usura não paga, o pagão!
    ═Orelha ursos tragam,
        Se afagam,
Mammumma, mammumma, Mammão.

(Magnetico *handle-organ*; *ring* d'ursos sentenciando á
pena-última o architecto da Pharsalia; odysseu
phantasma nas chammas dos incendios d'Albion:)

—Bear. . . Bear é ber'beri, Bear. . . Bear. . .
═Mammumma, mammumma, Mammão!
    —Bear. . . Bear. . . ber'. . . Pegàsus. . .
        Parnasus. . .
═Mammumma, mammumma, Mammão.

JOAQUIM DE SOUSÂNDRADE

(Washington 'blinding because of them'; Pocahontas
            without *personals*:)

> —To starving bears, a rabid dog!
> Be it! After the feast, bring in festoons! . .
>   =Tender Lulu,
>   Crying and you
>   Give honey to 'foes', bee? . . . and sting poltroons?

(Guatemalan nose, curved into Hymenee's torch; Dame-
      Ryder heart on the poisoned window-panes *of the
      'too dark' wedding pudding:*)

> —'Caramba! yo soy cirujano—
> A Jesuit . . . Yankee . . . industrialism'!
>   —*Job* . . . or haunted cavern,
>   Tavern,
> 'Byron' beastly-magnetism! . .

(Practical swindlers doing their business; *self-help*
            Atta-Troll:)

> —Let the foreigner fall helpless,
> As usury won't pay, the pagan!
>   =An ear to the bears a feast,
>   Caressing beasts,
>   Mahmmuhmmah, mahmmuhmmah, Mammon.

(Magnetic *handle-organ; ring* of bears sentencing the
      architect of the Pharsalia to death; an Odyssean
      ghost amidst the flames of Albion's fires:)

> —Bear . . . Bear is beriberi, Bear . . . Bear . . .
>   Mahmmuhmmah, mahmmuhmmah, Mammon!
>   —Bear . . . Bear . . . ber' . . . Pegasus
>   Parnassus
>   =Mahmmuhmmah, mahmmuhmmah, Mammon.

translated from Portuguese by
ODILE CISNEROS

九句

土雛や鼻の先だけ暮残る
tsuchibina ya hana no saki dake kure nokoru

○

遅桜卵を破れば腐り居る
ososakura tamago o yabureba kusari oru

○

水打てば御城下町の匂かな
mizu uteba gojōkamachi no nioi kana

○

かへり見る頰の肥りよ杏いろ
kaerimiru hoho no futari yo anzu iro

○

かげろふや猫にのまるる水たまり
kagerō ya neko ni nomaruru mizutamari

(continued)

Nine Haiku

clay dolls—
only the tips of their noses
are left in the dark

O

late cherry blossoms—
when i crack the egg
it's rotten

O

as rain hits
the great castle town,
its odors

O

looking back
your cheeks are fat
the color of apricots

O

heat shimmer...
a cat drinking
a puddle

(continued)

昼の月霍乱人が眼ざしやな
hiru no tsuki kakuran hito ga manazashi ya na

○

木がらしや目刺しにのこる海の色
kogarashi ya mezashi ni nokoru umi no iro

○

惣嫁指の白きも葱に似たりけり
sō ka yubi no shiroki mo negi ni nitari keri

○

水洟や鼻の先だけ暮残る
mizubana ya hana no saki dake kure nokoru

AKUTAGAWA RYŪNOSUKE

daytime moon
a person sick with heat
gives me a look

O

cold winter gusts—
on dried sardines remains
the sea's color

O

all young wives'
white fingers resemble
spring onions

O

His Last Haiku:

runny nose
its tip is all that's left
in this dark

translated from Japanese by
SEAN PRICE

Chlora Marx (Curriculum vitae)

Chlora Marx est une fille métallique aux cheveux générateurs d'effluves toxiques.
Elle expérimente les raisonnements de type 1 sans savoir pourquoi.
C'est dans le doute et la survie qu'elle continue d'appeler ce qu'elle croit sa mission.
Elle n'obtient jamais de réponse.

Son calvaire commence dans les entrailles d'un aéroport : elle se déguise en infirmière pour prendre en comptes les émotions les plus intimes de tous les voyageurs y compris les siennes.
Puis elle prétend être étudiante sur les campus, devient Pom Pom girl et serial killer en un minimum de temps sans jamais avoir suivi une leçon.
Sa dernière activité est la décomposition des instants passés, présents et à venir de sa vie, arrêts sur images puis ralentis, pour revivre les moments intenses.
Elle s'allonge sur un lit puis s'engage totalement dans l'événement vécu, une "surintoxication" des neurones. L'exercice requiert une extrême acuité des sensations : visualiser une scène depuis plusieurs angles de vue, utiliser pour cela des outils technologiques, revêtir un casque sur la tête, des lunettes virtuelles et actionner les commandes d'un "jeu" inédit, consacré entièrement au déroulement seconde par seconde de sa propre vie. Explorer chaque action avec exagération.
Le mode d'emploi suggère de :
—Réveiller son agressivité naturelle
—Convoiter l'inefficacité en tant que valeur humaine.
—Augmenter sa sensibilité par un entraînement intensif.
—Appréhender l'activisme individuel à travers ses perceptions sensorielles et l'analyse de son environnement.
—Choisir ses préférences visuelles dans un monde survisualisé.

Chlora vit de ses symptômes et parle 8 langues étrangères.
Hobbies : none
Objets de délits : elle est passée par sa phase "normalisante" dans un "monde de fous", elle décide à présent de se reconnecter avec son "moi" profond, sa "légende personnelle".

Les repères ont sautés depuis des millénaires, il va falloir affronter les heures prochaines sans idéologie de base, sans croyance, sans certitudes et sans émotions.
L'être humain régie son propre thermostat.
La chair est faible, impure à la consommation. Il faut renoncer.
D'où l'impression de flou et d'isolement thermique.
D'où l'idée de...

Chlora décide donc malgré tout de s'immerger dans le "retour du Jedi".
Evasion manquée de peu parceque peu d'entraînement :
[Ce qui est dit ne me dit rien]

SANDRA MOUSSEMPÈS

Chlora Marx (Curriculum vitae)

Chlora Marx is a metal girl with hair generated from toxic rivers.

She experiments with type 1 reasoning without knowing why.

In doubting and in surviving she keeps calling out what she believes to be her mission. She never gets an answer.

Her cavalry begins in the bowels of an airport: She disguises herself as a nurse in order to record the travelers' most intimate emotions. She understands them.

Then on campus she pretends to be a student, and in no time becomes a pom pom girl and serial killer without even taking classes.

Her last activity is to de-compose passing time, those present and those to come, in her life. She stops certain images, then slows them down, in order to relive intense moments.

She stretches out on the bed, totally tuned into live events, an "overintoxication" of neurons. This exercise requires that she be acutely aware of each sensation: visualize a scene from multiple points of view. To do this she will use technology, wear a helmet, vr glasses, and initiate certain commands in the newly released "this is your life game" which is programmed exclusively to unwind her entire life second by second. Explore each action with exaggeration.

The instructions suggest:

—That she revive animal instincts

—Covet ineffectiveness as a desirable human trait

—Heighten sensibility through intense training

—Apprehend individual activism through sensory perceptions and an analysis of her environment

—Choose visual preferences from the image-saturated world

Chlora lives in her symptoms and speaks eight languages.

Hobbies: none

Offenses: having passed through the "normalizing" phase in the "crazy world" she decides to reconnect with her profound "I", her "personal mythology."

States of mind that were shattered for a million years now must face the hours that follow without an ideological base, without belief, without certainty and without emotion.

The human being maintains an average temperature.

Flesh is weak, impure at conception. Renounce it.

Where did fuzzy impressions and thermal isolation come from.

Where did the idea that . . .

In spite of it all Chlora decided to become immersed in "The Return of the Jedi."

Escaped just barely because of hardly any training:

[What was said means nothing to me].

translated from French by
KRISTIN PREVALLET

Gobice

I

Bila je blazna vročina
to moram namreč povedati
hodimo v čredi kot govedo
nekateri pobožni
nekateri pa tudi ne
kot pač koga prime

On pourrait bien y mettre un taxi
debela Tevtonka pade pa kar skupaj
MOLČE
to mi je blazno všeč taka resnost

Bila je blazna vročina
to moram namreč povedati

Sine se pa pelje v kočiji za dvesto lir
C'est quand même drôle tout ça
in že se prikaže sv. Frančišek s ptički
izstopi iz konzerve Simmenthal in zapre pokrov
poverello con suoi occhi ingenui
blazno mi je všeč
ta poslednji konstruktivni tip
v evropski zgodovini

Bila je blazna vročina
to moram namreč povedati

II

Namreč tako je z vso to zadevo
najboljše stvari so gobice
gobice v juhi
nič nič nič nič

                    fiuuuuu ena gobica
en zelen peteršiljček v smokingu
pa dolgo dolgo časa tema

(continued)

Little Mushrooms

I

It was immensely hot
this I must tell you

We walk in a herd like cattle
some devout
some not so
as one's whimsy goes

They should put a taxi here
the fat Teutoness fades away
TACITLY
I love this kind of seriousness

It was immensely hot
this I must tell you

Sonny drives around in a carriage for two hundred lira
c'est quand meme drole tout ca
and St. Francis appears with his birds
steps out of the can and closes the lid
poverello con suoi occhi ingenui
amazing how much I like
this last constructive chap
in the history of Europe

It was immensely hot
this I must tell you

II

So it goes
best of all are the little mushrooms
little mushrooms in the soup
nothing nothing nothing nothing

                      pheeooooo one little mushroom

one green parsley in tuxedo
then darkness for a long long time   *(continued)*

potem stečejo po snažilko
ki je za vse to odgovorna
nič nič nič nič
                fiuuuuu še ena gobica
zdrava sicer
le kri ni ena A
ker je prebolela hepatitis
Težke so težke te gobice
težke v božjo mater

III

Odstranili bomo čevlje z gumo
zakaj takih se več ne nosi
in smrt in muhe
ki nimajo urejenih pristanišč

odstranili bomo nekatera neumna števila
tako da bomo končno lahko zadihali
in svobodno šteli
ena dva tri sedemnajst
odstranili bomo vse besede
ki imajo manj kot pet črk
zakaj popolnoma jasno je
da se take besede samo valjajo
in planine

odstranili bom krog
ker imamo kvadrat
ker zakaj bi imel človek
eno nogo takšno
in drugo nogo takšno
in popoldne
ker takrat sonce zahaja

odstranili bomo vranico
ker kaj bi z vranico
ko pa imamo jetra pljuča
in sploh preveč teh stvari
in Sicilijo
ker je navaden patološki pojav
linolej
ker ne ve kje leži Baku

(continued)

then they run to find a cleaner
responsible for everything
nothing nothing nothing nothing

                pheeooooo one little mushroom more

healthy though
except the blood is not grade a
it recovered from hepatitis
Heavy, heavy are these little mushrooms
heavy Holy Mother o' God!

III

We'll do away with rubber shoes
because we don't have them anymore
and death and flies
without their ports in order

We'll do away with some silly numbers
so we can finally begin to breathe
and count freely
one two three seventeen
We'll do away with all words
five letters or less
because it's so clear
these words only roll
and highlands

We'll do away with circle
because we have square
because why should man have
one leg like this
and a second like this
and afternoon
because the sun goes down

We'll do away with the spleen
because what should we do with the spleen
when we have liver lungs
and too many of these things
and Sicily
because it's a plain pathological phenomenon
linoleum
because it doesn't know where Baku is

(continued)

in sviterje ki se oblačijo čez glavo
odstranili bomo dihanje

                    ker se udira
                    ker se udira
                    ker se udira

in konopljo
ker lan in konoplja
to se blazno čudno sliši

odstranili bomo nebo
in vodo ker se začne na V
in le poglejte ta znak
kako balansira na eni nogi
in zeva proti vrhu

in nazadnje čas
in sploh čistočo
zakaj vsaka čistoča se zamaže
in kaj potem kaj potem

IV

Brez tebe črka P gre k vragu svet
paradajs pasma politika
ali ste že videli papagaja brez črle P
ali pa pipico pokaditi Pennsylvania
brez tebe črka P ostane
žavbica akvamarin nastlati namazati
vse pa sloni na pakeljcih
poglejmo samo težave
ki nastopijo v zemljepisu
hodiš po svetu prideš do Patagonije
stop črna luknja
niti ne moreš vzeti palice
da bi jo naslonil
na pred-Patagonijo in po-Patagonijo
pa se ti zabliska pa rečeš TRAM
pa še TRAM ti pade v luknjo
ker ni pakeljcev
nikoli ne ješ po naročilu
zmeraj žvečiš menu
potem hočeš spat a samo zehaš
in zehaš nag ker pidžame ni
tako se razvije nemorala
tako se razvije nemorala
perutnice poštarji pamtivek

(continued)

and sweatshirts because we pull them over our heads
we'll do away with breathing
                          because it stinks
                          because it stinks
                          because it stinks
and hemp
because linen and hemp
it sounds awfully strange

We'll do away with sky
and valley because it starts with V
just look at it
how it balances on one leg
and yawns upward

and finally, time
and cleanliness
because all cleanliness gets dirty
and then what, then what

IV

Without you letter P the world goes to hell
pomegranate pedigree politics
did you ever see a parrot without the letter P
or a pipe plumber, Pennsylvania
without the letter P we still have
little balm aquamarine to strew to spread
but everything leans on a plank
let's look at the hassle
which happens in geography
you walk through the world and come to Patagonia
stop at a black hole
you can't even take a pole
to lean on to
pre-Patagonian and post-Patagonian
you get it in a flash and say BEAM
or even the Beam falls into a hole
because there are no planks
you never eat a la carte
but always chew the menu
you want to go to sleep but you only yawn
but you yawn naked because you have no pajamas
this is how unchastity develops
this is how unchastity develops
postmasters particles pre-pasture times

(continued)

V

Čudno se mi potapljaš kenguru
in če ti ponudim slamico
me samo vlažno gledaš

nikoli nisi razmišljal
zakaj krave ne vzniknejo
ampak se zmeraj rodijo
kot teleta kenguru

blazno lepo si splaval
to je res
vendar so bile neke sence
že od rojstva
gorgonzole nisi jedel
imel si lase na blazinicah
in nekaj rikiki
je bilo v tem kako si se obrnil
ali se sploh zavedaš
da je bil Caravaggio psihopat
da je jokal če je videl redkvice
a kje je pot na Krim kenguru

kradel si nam čevlje
zvrnil bekačin
šnite si hotel delati iz časa
a čas je zmeraj čas
samo da je v senci
sprime se ob pravi uri kenguru

poskusiva reči Victor Hugo
Victor Hugo
no no vidiš da gre
ali bi lahko tudi rekla Esplanade

tako je kot sem si mislil kenguru
nimaš ravno tifusa
ampak tudi ni dosti boljše
čudno se mi potapljaš kenguru
tudi če bi ti vrgel traktor
stavim da bi ga olupil in pojedel
ampak traktor ni za to kenguru
traktor je za to
da poskusiš priti iz vode
olupi in poje se jabolko

(continued)

V

It's strange how you sink, kangaroo
and if I show you a straw
you mostly only stare at me

you never thought
why cows do not sprout
but are always born
as calves, kangaroo

cool when you learned to swim
that's a fact
but some shadows were there
from the day of your birth
you didn't eat gorgonzola
there was hair on your fingertips
and something cockadoodledo
was in how you turned around,
were you at all aware,
Caravaggio was a psychopath
cried each time he saw a radish
But where's the way to Mt. Crim, kangaroo

you stole our shoes
you turned around a snipe
you wanted to make slices from time
but time is always time
only, it's in the shadow
it sticks together at the right hour, kangaroo

let's try to say Victor Hugo
Victor Hugo
you see you see it works
could we say also Esplanade

so it is as I thought kangaroo
you may not have typhus exactly
but it's not much better
it's strange how you sink kangaroo
even if I threw you a tractor
I bet you would peel and eat it
but a tractor is not for that kangaroo
a tractor is how one gets
from the water
we peel and eat an apple

(continued)

ali naj pokličem sorodnike kenguru
ali si želiš biti vdova pol oboka
ali v slogi je moč kenguru
ali naj ti kaj zapojem
ali naj ti zapojem
quand un pompier
rencontre un autre pompier

nič ti ne bom zapel kenguru
zakaj tako pesem bodo prepevali
tvoji sovražniki
ker taki so pač sovražniki
da prepevajo take pesmi

VI

> The 'potamus can never reach
> The mango on the mango-tree
> (T. S. Eliot, *The Hippopotamus*)

S sirom hranimo se zjutraj ali po obedu
Je regrette l'Europe aux ancien parapets
zgodovino delajo napredni
No to je ravno tisto kar je najbolj razveseljivo

Bradlja Hegel rožice v naravi
trije so pojavi stvarstva
Mojzes padel iz plenic v zgodovino
v sivih dokolenkah čaka na propad zapada

Strpnost vera v znanost ribe v morju
tvorijo sveta bleščavo
žakelj žakelj žakelj žakelj
PRIHOD IZ ŽAKLJA DRUGO POGLAVJE

TOMAŽ ŠALAMUN

shall I call your relatives, kangaroo
do you want to be a window, half of an arch
strength in numbers, kangaroo
shall I sing you something
shall I sing to you
quand un pompier
recontre un autre pompier

I will not sing you anything, kangaroo
because such a song will be sung
by your enemies
because so are the enemies
to sing such songs

VI

> The 'potamus can never reach
> The mango on the mango tree
> (T.S. Eliot, *The Hippopotamus*)

We feed ourselves with cheese in the morning or after the meal
Je regrette l'Europe aux anciens parapets
history is made by the progressive ones
Well, this is what seems the most agreeable

Parallel bars Hegel little flowers in nature
are three phenomena of the universe
Moses, fell from diapers into history
and in gray socks waits for the West to collapse

Tolerance trust in science fish in water
make the world's perfect glitter
the sack the sack the sack the sack
COMING OUT OF THE SACK THE SECOND CHAPTER

translated from Slovenian by
JOSHUA BECKMAN & TOMAŽ ŠALAMUN

詩畢後再題一絕

事難如志都歸命
詩豈酬恩略表心
回首河山人宛在
相思便作幾回吟

YÜAN MEI

Finished with a parting poem for Mr. Li I went on to write this shorter one

Life is harder than our dreams,
but both at last come down to chance.
Poems repay no debts . . .
They may but show a little of the heart.
When I turned to look back at the river and the hills,
words from *The Book of Odes* came to me:
"Lo, he is right in the middle of the waters . . ."
and thinking of you, I chanted them once,
and then once again.

translated from Chinese by
J. P. SEATON

丈洲

身非鳧雁水為家
日日輕蓬傍淺沙
蘆荻也知官吏到
隨風吹送滿船花

YÜAN MEI

124

Chang-chou

I'm not such a goose that I live on the water . . .
but day after day my light sail has glided through the shallows.
Even the reeds know a Great Official's here.
Following the winds of custom
they see me off
                    with a <u>boatful</u> of blossoms.

translated from Chinese by
J. P. SEATON

答孟亭訊梅

寒梅初種後
曾與故人期
待放一林雪
各吟千首詩
忽來連夜雨
凍斷早春枝
自是花渝約
非關沽酒遲

YÜAN MEI

Meng-t'ing Asked about Plum Blossoms, and I Answered

After I planted these chill-plums
I set a rendezvous with you:
"Wait until they blossom, groves of snow," said I
"and we'll each chant a thousand verses."
Now comes all-night rain
to freeze, to break each early spray of Spring.
Ah, but since the flowers stood us up,
it's no matter I forgot to buy the wine.

translated from Chinese by
J. P. SEATON

Take Two:
"On the Subject of Flowers:
Remarks, Addressed to the Poet"

A rthur Rimbaud's *"Ce qu'on dit au poet à propos des fleurs"* appears in a letter the sixteen-year old wrote to Théodore de Banville, a respected Parisian poet of the day. The letter was Rimbaud's second to Banville. In his first, Rimbaud had written with the hope the elder would offer some form of encouragement or assistance. Although we do not know the particulars of Banville's response, it is certain that no assistance was forthcoming, whatever encouragement might have been offered.

The second letter, sent a year later, asks, cheekily, "Have I improved?" It is an interesting question, particularly given the nature of the poem Rimbaud includes.

A barbed parody of the sort of poetry Banville himself was writing, the poem is 160 rhymed lines of gentle invective, a highly-cheeky sort of hello, an excellent way of getting attention, but not necessarily the best way of getting in Banville's graces.

This is my second translation of the poem. The first appeared in *Rimbaud Complete* (Modern Library, 2002). The new version was occasioned by my edition of Rimbaud's correspondence, *I Promise to be Good* (Modern Library, 2003).

The two versions differ radically. The first is a very literal approach. The second, which follows, replicates Rimbaud's rhyme scheme, something I did not attempt the first time out. As the poem itself is, in French, useful only inasmuch as it refers to conventions of the day, it is highly perishable. To translate the poem literally and without rhyme is to lose whatever limited charm it may possess.

In this new version, I have seen to approach the lines with considerably more liberty than before.

WYATT MASON

Ce qu'on dit au Poète
à propos de fleurs

À monsieur Théodore de Banville

I

Ainsi, toujours, vers l'azur noir
Où tremble la mer des topazes,
Fonctionneront dans ton soir
Les Lys, ces clystères d'extases!

A notre époque de sagous,
Quand les Plantes sont travailleuses,
Le Lys boira les bleus dégoûts
Dans tes Proses religieuses!

—Le lys de monsieur de Kerdrel,
Le Sonnet de mil huit cent trente,
Le Lys qu'on donne au Ménestrel
Avec l'œillet et l'amarante!

Des lys! Des lys! On n'en voit pas!
Et dans ton Vers, tel que les manches
Des Pécheresses aux doux pas,
Toujours frissonnent ces fleurs blanches!

Toujours, Cher, quand tu prends un bain,
Ta Chemise aux aisselles blondes
Se gonfle aux brises du matin
Sur les myosotis immondes!

L'amour ne passe à tes octrois
Que les Lilas,—ô balançoires!
Et les Violettes du Bois,
Crachats sucrés des Nymphes noires!...

II

Ô Poètes, quand vous auriez
Les Roses, les Roses soufflées,
Rouges sur tiges de lauriers,
Et de mille octaves enflées!

(continued)

On the Subject of Flowers:
Remarks, Addressed to the Poet

To Monsieur Théodore de Banville

I

There, bordering blue black skies
Where wavecrests tremble gold,
Lilies stimulate evening ecstasies,
Enemas thrust between bardic folds.

After all, times have changed:
Plants now labor—aloe and rose.
Lilies artfully arranged
Decorate your religious prose.

Kerdrel disappeared behind them
In the Sonnet of eighteen-thirty;
Poets are buried beneath them,
In amaranth and carnation flurries.

Lilies, lilies. So often mentioned,
So seldom seen. In your verses, though
They blossom like good intentions
As sinners' resolutions come and go.

Why, even when you bathe, Dear Sir,
Your sallow-pitted gown must bloom
With morning breezes: sleeves confer
High above forget-me-nots in swoon.

Yes: our garden gates let lilacs pass.
But such candied clichés have a cost:
Pollinating spit on petals looks like glass
But is still spit. Our poor flowers? Lost.

II

And when you get your hands on roses,
Windwhipped roses red on laurel stems,
Their effect upon you one supposes
Irresistible: bad verses just never end.

(continued)

Quand BANVILLE en ferait neiger,
Sanguinolentes, tournoyantes,
Pochant l'œil fou de l'étranger
Aux lectures mal bienveillantes!

De vos forêts et de vos prés,
Ô très paisibles photographes!
La Flore est diverse à peu près
Comme des bouchons de carafes!

Toujours les végétaux Français,
Hargneux, phtisiques, ridicules,
Où le ventre des chiens bassets
Navigue en paix, aux crépuscules;

Toujours, après d'affreux desseins
De Lotos bleus ou d'Hélianthes,
Estampes roses, sujets saints
Pour de jeunes communiantes!

L'Ode Açoka cadre avec la
Strophe en fenêtre de lorette;
Et de lourds papillons d'éclat
Fientent sur la Pâquerette.

Vieilles verdures, vieux galons!
Ô croquignoles végétales!
Fleurs fantasques des vieux Salons!
—Aux hannetons, pas aux crotales,

Ces poupards végétaux en pleurs
Que Grandville eût mis aux lisières,
Et qu'allaitèrent de couleurs
De méchants astres à visières!

Oui, vos bavures de pipeaux
Font de précieuses glucoses!
—Tas d'œufs frits dans de vieux chapeaux,
Lys, Açokas, Lilas et Roses!...

III

Ô blanc Chasseur, qui cours sans bas
A travers le Pâtis panique,
Ne peux tu pas, ne dois—tu pas
Connaître un peu ta botanique?

(continued)

BANVILLE's roses fall like snow,
Their whiteness flecked with blood.
A pricking feeling readers know:
Incomprehension chafes and rubs.

Through grassy banks and wooded ways
Feast your shutterbugging eyes.
What they seize on sure amazes:
A monotony of pretty lies.

Why this mania for floral arranging?
Why does it prompt such turgid lines?
Low-slung hounds with bellies dangling
French poets are tickled by muddy vines.

As if the lines weren't bad enough,
Consider the pictures they adjoin...
A first communion? Either option's rough:
Sunflowers or Lotuses? Flip a coin.

Can French poets resist an Ashokan ode?
Can addicts resist a free bag of blow?
As if butterflies take the high road,
To avoid shitting on daisies below.

All this greenery is becoming mulch.
Blossoms plucked to raise the stakes.
Salons bedecked like a flowery gulch
Better for beetles than rattlesnakes.

Grandville's sentimental sketchings
Fill margins with mawkish blooms,
Caricatures of flowery retchings
Evening stars the dark consumes.

Saliva drooling from your pipings
Is all we have for nectar: Pan now dozes.
His song has become mere guttersniping
About Lilies, Ashokas, Lilacs, Roses.

III

O White Hunters: your barefoot excursions
Trample the pastoral into derision;
Shouldn't your flowery poetic diversions
Exhibit a modicum of botanical precision?

(continued)

Tu ferais succéder, je crains,
Aux Grillons roux les Cantharides,
L'or des Rios au bleu des Rhins—
Bref, aux Norwèges les Florides:

Mais, Cher, l'Art n'est plus, maintenant,
—C'est la vérité,—de permettre
A l'Eucalyptus étonnant
Des constrictors d'un hexamètre;

Là!... Comme si les Acajous
Ne servaient, même en nos Guyanes,
Qu'aux cascades des sapajous,
Au lourd délire des lianes!

—En somme, une Fleur, Romarin
Ou Lys, vive ou morte, vaut-elle
Un excrément d'oiseau marin?
Vaut-elle un seul pleur de chandelle?

—Et j'ai dit ce que je voulais!
Toi, même assis là-bas, dans une
Cabane de bambous,—volets
Clos, tentures de perse brune—

Tu torcherais des floraisons
Dignes d'Oises extravagantes!...
—Poète! ce sont des raisons
Non moins risibles qu'arrogantes!...

IV

Dis, non les pampas printaniers
Noirs d'épouvantables révoltes,
Mais les tabacs, les cotonniers!
Dis les exotiques récoltes!

Dis, front blanc que Phébus tanna,
De combien de dollars se rente
Pedro Velasquez, Habana;
Incague la mer de Sorrente

Où vont les Cygnes par milliers;
Que tes strophes soient des réclames
Pour l'abatis des mangliers
Fouillés des hydres et des lames!

(continued)

You deploy Crickets and Flies indiscriminately
Conflating Phylum and Genus. Rio's gold
And Rhine's blue are switched inadvertently,
Poor Norway becomes "Florida, but cold."

In the past, Dear Master, Art may have settled
For the alexandrine's hexametrical constrictions;
But now, shouldn't the stink of fallen petals
Rotting, make a clean sweep of our ambitions?

Our botanically-challenged bards forever bungle:
Mahogany is "a flower found in the country:"
Who could imagine that in the Guyan jungle
The real trees support armies of monkeys?

If decadent decoration is the answer that looms
To prettify your pages, the larger question's clear:
Is this riotous, ceaseless, vomitation of blooms
Worth a seagull's turd or one candle's tear?

I think I've made my point: sitting there,
A poet in his far-flung bamboo hut,
Draped with Persian rugs in the Sahara,
You resolutely keep the shutters shut:

And then describe the sands as full
Of flowers, ignoring barren dunes:
This sort of thing—so disgraceful—is bull.
Keep it up, and drive poetry to its doom.

IV

Heard of the notion of "keeping it real"?
Your efforts until now have been rotten.
Enough of this milk-fed literary veal:
Try describing tobacco and cotton.

Why not render Pedro Velazquez' face
And the dollars his cash-crop brings;
Let sun brown skin, your pallor erase,
Describe the shit on swans' white wings:

Yes: the Sorrento sea is full of feathers,
But an ocean of crap floats there too;
Are your stanzas equipped for all weathers?
Are there hydras in the waters with you?

(continued)

Ton quatrain plonge aux bois sanglants
Et revient proposer aux Hommes
Divers sujets de sucres blancs,
De pectoraires et de gommes!

Sachons par Toi si les blondeurs
Des Pics neigeux, vers les Tropiques,
Sont ou des insectes pondeurs
Ou des lichens microscopiques!

Trouve, ô Chasseur, nous le voulons,
Quelques garances parfumées
Que la Nature en pantalons
Fasse éclore!—pour nos Armées!

Trouve, aux abords du Bois qui dort,
Les fleurs, pareilles à des mufles,
D'où bavent des pommades d'or
Sur les cheveux sombres des Buffles!

Trouve, aux prés fous, où sur le Bleu
Tremble l'argent des pubescences,
Des Calices pleins d'Œufs de feu
Qui cuisent parmi les essences!

Trouve des Chardons cotonneux
Dont dix nes aux yeux de braises
Travaillent à filer les noeuds!
Trouve des Fleurs qui soient des chaises!

Oui, trouve au coeur des noirs filons
Des fleurs presque pierres,—fameuses!—
Qui vers leurs durs ovaires blonds
Aient des amygdales gemmeuses!

Sers-nous, ô Farceur, tu le peux,
Sur un plat de vermeil splendide
Des ragouts de Lys sirupeux
Mordant nos cuillers Alfénide!

    V

Quelqu'un dira le grand Amour,
Voleur des sombres Indulgences:
Mais ni Renan, ni le chat Murr
N'ont vu les Bleus Thyrses immenses!

(continued)

Thrust quatrains into the bloody woods
And report the news that we need.
Expostulate on sugar and durable goods
Whether pansements or rubbers that bleed.

Your job? Deliver truth on these matters,
Such as what covers our tropical peaks;
Is what crowns them like snow-scatters
Lichen, or eggs from insectoid beaks?

O White Hunters, we really must insist
You find us perfumed madders' hues;
Nature nurtures, we gather: fat fists
Dye the trousers infantrymen abuse.

Find flowers that look like muzzles,
At forest fringes dead with sleep;
Unpack oozing botanical puzzles,
Ochre ointments that they leak.

Find calyxes full of fiery eggs
Cooking in aestival juices
In meadows gone insane with legs:
Pubescent insects Spring seduces.

Find cottony thistledown in bunches
By which donkeys' vision is impaired.
Nature never pulls her punches,
Some flowers even look like chairs.

Yes: find in the heart of dark divides
Flowers that look like precious gems;
Pistols and stamens the darkness hides
But crystally encrusts with faceted hems.

For once—Sad Jester—just serve it up;
Lay our table with a purple platter.
Fill it with a lily stew's sweet syrup:
Fill our spoons with the heart of the matter.

V

And, of course, we now arrive at *love*:
Surely it should be the poet's thing.
Yet Renan below and Murr above
Avoid all Dionysian blossoming.

(continued)

Toi, fais jouer dans nos torpeurs,
Par les parfums les hystéries;
Exalte-nous vers des candeurs
Plus candides que les Maries...

Commerçant! colon! médium!
Ta Rime sourdra, rose ou blanche,
Comme un rayon de sodium,
Comme un caoutchouc qui s'épanche!

De tes noirs Poèmes,—Jongleur!
Blancs, verts, et rouges dioptriques,
Que s'évadent d'étranges fleurs
Et des papillons électriques!

Voilà! c'est le Siècle d'enfer!
Et les poteaux télégraphiques
Vont orner,—lyre aux chants de fer,
Tes omoplates magnifiques!

Surtout, rime une version
Sur le mal des pommes de terre!
—Et, pour la composition
De Poèmes pleins de mystères

Qu'on doive lire de Tréguier
A Paramaribo, rachète
Des Tomes de Monsieur Figuier,
—Illustrés!—chez Monsieur Hachette!

Alcide Bava
A.R.
14 juillet 1871

ARTHUR RIMBAUD

Put your perfumes to good use:
Scent our stink of torpid lust;
Redeem the wanting we produce,
Lift us heavenward on verbal gusts.

Let *practicality* be a poetic criterion,
As for any Soldier, Psychic or Salesman.
Awake us from thiopentalic delirium
Split us like rubber trees: tear us open.

Let strange fruit fall from stanzas,
Prismatic light refract from verses;
Black wings, lepidoptric memorandas,
Flutterings full of electric purpose.

An Age of Hell is now upon us:
The earthly body pierced with spears.
Telegraphic poles limn each Gowanus
Helplessly broadcasting silent tears.

Spin, my poet, a tale of terrestrial blight,
Exalt, somehow, in the potato's sorry life;
Rhyme all ruin to make wrong right
Feed your poems on earthly strife—

Whether in Babylon or Bayonne—
Let them ramble, let them range
Over paper like low moans:
Graze the poem: make it strange.

> *Alcide Bava*
> *A.R.*
> *July 14, 1871*

translated from French by
WYATT MASON

馬の話

村のはずれで
粥を食べている女も馬の話
色付きジュースの好きな子どもも馬の話
とおく池のなかでは
石を抱いて馬の話を聞いておくれ
馬の話を聞いておくれ
糞にまじるタバコを噛んで騒いでやまない馬
馬は今日と明日の間で深深といななく
馬の満月

村人たちが馬の話をもとめるから
崖のように直立している馬
屋根に馬の虹が架かるので映らなくなるテレビ
村人たちが馬の話をもとめるから
タバコ畑の一方から押寄せる馬の胞衣の洪水
その年から年じゅうの暴動には
村人たちはいつも丁寧におどろいてやまない
（その陳腐さを想像できる?）

かれらは高窓からシーツを垂らしてなおも叫ぶ
馬の話をしたい!
馬の話だ
たった　ひとつ馬の話だ
すると
畝の間から火のついた馬が駈け出してくる
かれらは自分自身が馬の姿形をしていたことに
ついに本当におどろく
恐慌する村人たちの
赤いたてがみの堰
さあ馬の話をはじめよう!

TAKARABE TORIKO

Talk of Horses

A woman eating gruel at the end of the village
also talks of horses.
A child who likes colored juice also talks of horses.
Far away, in a pond,
a man holding a stone in his arms never stops talking of horses.
Listen to my talk of horses.
A horse that has chewed tobacco in the straw doesn't stop struggling.
Horses neigh deeply, deeply between today and tomorrow.
A horse's full moon.
Because the villagers want talks of horses,
the horses stand erect as a cliff.
Because a rainbow of horses hangs over the roof the TV stops working.
Because villagers want talks of horses,
from one end of the tobacco field surges a flood of horses' afterbirths.
Their riots year in year out
never stop politely surprising the villagers.
(Can you imagine that cliché?)
They hang sheets from high windows and shout:
We want to talk of horses!
I wanted to talk of horses.
Just one talk of horses.
Then
from a paddy ridge flaming horses gallop out.
They are finally truly surprised
that they themselves are horse-shaped.
The awe-struck villagers
make a dam of red manes.
Now let's talk of horses!

translated from Japanese by
HIROAKI SATO

Male Dicat

(în fiecare noapte înainte de a
stinge lumina intru în bucătărie
cu gîndul să dau drumul la gaz
pînă la urmă dau drumul la apă
iau un pahar îl clătesc apoi beau
şi mă clatin de silă mă gîndesc
"acolo în largul oceanului
pe o mare fîşie de cer nu a
zburat niciodată o pasăre")

CONSTANTIN ACOSMEI

Male Dicat

(every night before
shutting off the light I go into the kitchen
with the thought of turning on the gas
but instead I run the tap
take a glass rinse it drink it
and I shudder in disgust—I think
"there in the broad ocean,
on a large strip of sky
no bird has ever flown")

translated from Romanian by
GENE TANTA

רָאִיתָ אֶת הַגֶּשֶׁם? אֲנַחְנוּ שְׁקֵטִים.
שְׁלֹשָׁה מַלְאָכִים מִסִּפּוּר עַתִּיק
הוֹלְכִים לְאִטָּם בֵּין עֵצִים וּבָתִּים.

דָּבָר לֹא שֻׁנָּה. רַק הַגֶּשֶׁם מַקְשִׁיב
בְּזָהֳרוּת עַל הָאֶבֶן. הָרְחוֹב מַבְרִיק.
אֲנַחְנוּ רוֹאִים אֵיךְ עוֹבְרִים אֶת הַכְּבִישׁ
שְׁלֹשָׁה מַלְאָכִים מִסִּפּוּר עַתִּיק.

הַדֶּלֶת פְּתוּחָה. הַסֻּלָּת בָּרָה.
הַגֶּשֶׁם שָׁקֵט, כִּי הַגַּס כְּבָר קָרָה.

LEA GOLDBERG

* *
 *

Have you seen the rain? We are calm.
Three angels from an ancient story
are moving slowly between the trees and homes.

Nothing has changed. Only the rain
is carefully hitting the stone. The street is glassy.
We see how three angels are crossing
the street from an ancient story.

The flour is pure. The door is open.
The rain is quiet. The miracle has already happened.

translated from Hebrew by
PETER COLE

עִם הַלַּיְלָה הַזֶּה

עִם הַלַּיְלָה הַזֶּה וְעִם כָּל שְׁתִיקוֹתָיו
עִם הַלַּיְלָה הַזֶּה –
עִם שְׁלֹשָׁה כּוֹכָבִים
שֶׁאָבְדוּ בֵּין עֵצִים
עִם הָרוּחַ הַזֹּאת.

עִם הָרוּחַ הַזֹּאת
שֶׁעָמְדָה לְהַקְשִׁיב
לַלַּיְלָה הַזֶּה –
עִם הַלַּיְלָה הַזֶּה
וּשְׁלֹשָׁה כּוֹכָבִים
וְהָרוּחַ הַזֹּאת.

LEA GOLDBERG

With This Night

With this night and all its silence
with this night—
with three stars
lost among trees
with this wind.

With this wind
stopped to listen
to this night—
with this night
and three stars,
and this wind.

translated from Hebrew by
PETER COLE

Presagios

En homenaje a Elizabeth Bishop

1

Las nubes se deslizan a tal velocidad
que impiden ir en pos del día,
seguir sus huellas,
hablarle por su nombre.
¿Cómo te llamas?, pregunté.
No hubo respuesta.
Sí, en cambio, un alboroto inmenso.
Aproveché una pieza del mosaico,
sus grises, blancos, metálicos matices,
un momento de mi vida.
Y salí a su encuentro.
Era tan bello.
La poca bruma, desprovista,
se iba dispersando poco a poco
al ritmo de un radiante corazón
que no podía ser el mío.
Fugaces ya, las fuerzas intentaron huir también,
pero el coro unánime del clima las retuvo
a punto de olvidarse
y nunca más hallar cabida en la ilusión,
a las puertas
de la tierra
de la abundancia.
Qué solar misericordia.

2

Sublime,
se desborda este caudal
al compartirse.

Como quien lleva una canasta
con lo mejor de la estación,
deseos renuentes,
agua profunda, antigua,
nacida tras la piedra
del cuerpo que respira.

(continued)

Omens

In homage to Elizabeth Bishop

1

The clouds glide so slowly
they cannot go in pursuit of the day,
to follow its trail,
to call it by name.
What's your name? I asked.
There was no answer.
Yes, but a great disturbance.
I made use of a piece of the mosaic
its grays, whites, metallic shades,
a moment from my life.
And I left for the encounter.
He was so beautiful.
The little mist, lacking,
was dispersed little by little
to the beat of a radiant heart
that could not be mine.
Fleeting already, the forces tried also to flee,
but the unanimous chorus of the climate retained them
on the verge of forgetting themselves
and never finding space in the illusion,
to the doors
of the earth,
of its abundance.
What ancestral mercy.

2

Sublime,
overwhelmed with abundance
to partake.

Like one who carries a basket
containing the height of the season,
reluctant desires,
deep water, old,
born after the rock
of the body that breathes.

(continued)

Como quien toca el borde,
el horizonte de ese día,
con una gran necesidad
de recostarse donde sea,
y reconoce refulgente la canasta
de frutos propios, exquisitos.
Se sabe entonces convidado
a aquellas fiestas.
Se acerca al anfitrión.
Huele su túnica y sandalias,
su deslumbrante majestad.
Oye el latido de su sangre,
se mira dentro suyo
y da con todos los sentidos
en las cámaras secretas
de aquel *vivo* santuario.

Como quien dejara huella
y la borrara luego
con los ojos.

Como quien supiera adónde va,
y al dejar de ser
no fuera ya.

PURA LÓPEZ-COLOMÉ

Like one who touches the edge,
the horizon of day,
with one great need
to sit in place
and look upon the basket
gleaming with radiant fruit.
Who is known, then, as a guest
at those parties.
Who approaches the host.
Who smells his tunic and sandals,
his overwhelming majesty.
Who hears the beat of blood,
looks upon the soul
and discovers the senses
in the secret chambers
of that living sanctuary.

Like one who left a trail
and then erased it
with the eyes.

Like one who knew the path
and ceasing to be
was no longer.

translated from Spanish by
JASON STUMPF

Ang Sabi Ko Sa Iyo

Bumalong ang dagta
sa hiniwang kaymito.
Namuo sa talim
ng kutsilyo ang ilang patak.
Diyan ako naiwan, mahal,
at hindi sa laman.

BENILDA SANTOS

What I Told You

Nectar flowed
from the star-apple cut in half.
Drops formed
on the knife blade.
That was where I remained, love,
and not in the flesh.

translated from Filipino by
JOSÉ EDMUNDO OCAMPO REYES

Cumha Ghriogair MhicGhriogair Ghlinn Sreith

a dhìthcheannadh 'sa' bhliadhna 1570

Moch madainn air latha Lùnasd'
  Bha mi sùgradh mar ri m'ghràdh,
Ach mun tàinig meadhon latha
  Bha mo chridhe air a chràdh.

Ochain, ochain, ochain uiridh
  Is goirt mo chridhe, a laoigh,
Ochain, ochain, ochain uiridh
  Cha chluinn t'athair ar caoidh.

Mallachd aig maithibh is aig càirdean
  Rinn mo chràdh air an-dòigh,
Thàinig gun fhios air mo ghràdh-sa
  Is a thug fo smachd e le foill.

Nam biodh dà fhear dheug d'a chinneadh
  Is mo Ghriogair air an ceann,
Cha biodh mo shùil a' sileadh dheur,
  No mo leanabh féin gun dàimh.

Chuir iad a cheann air ploc daraich,
  Is dhòirt iad fhuil mu làr:
Nam biodh agam-sa an sin cupan.
  Dh'òlainn dith mo shàth.

Is truagh nach robh m'athair an galar,
  Agus Cailean Liath am plàigh,
Ged bhiodh nighean an Ruadhanaich
  Suathadh bas is làmh.

Chuirinn Cailean Liath fo ghlasaibh,
  Is Donnchadh Dubh an làimh;
'S gach Caimbeulach th'ann am Bealach
  Gu giùlan nan glas-làmh.

Ràinig mise réidhlean Bhealaich,
  Is cha d'fhuair mi ann tàmh:
Cha d'fhàg mi ròin de m'fhalt gun tarraing
  No craiceann air mo làimh.

(continued)

Elegy for Gregor MacGregor of Glenstrae

who was decapitated in the year 1570

Early morning, on the day of Lùnasda,[1]
    I was joking together with my love,
But before mid-day came
    My heart was being tormented.

Ochain, ochain, ochain uiridh
    My heart is mournful, my darling,
Ochain, ochain, ochain uiridh
    Your father will not hear our weeping.

A curse on the chieftains and friends
    Who caused me to be tortured like this,
Who came unbeknownst to my love
    And took him away, wrongfully arrested.

If there had been twelve men from his clan
    And my Gregor at their lead,
My eyes would not be raining tears,
    Nor my own children without kindred.

They put his head on an oak block,
    And they spilled his blood upon the ground:
If I could have had a cup
    I would have drunk my fill of it.[2]

It is a pity that my father was not sick
    And Colin Liath with plague
Although Lord Ruthven's daughter would be
    Wringing palm and hand.

I would lock up Colin Liath
    And put Duncan Dubh in custody
And every Campbell in Taymooth Castle
    Would be bearing manacles.

I reached the green of Taymooth Castle
    And I did not find rest there:
I did not leave a single one of my hairs unpulled
    Or any skin on my hand.

(continued)

Is truagh nach robh mi an riochd na h-uiseig,
  Spionnadh Ghriogair ann mo làimh:
Is i a' chlach a b'àirde anns a' chaisteal
  A' chlach a b'fhaisge do'n bhlàr.

Is ged tha mi gun ùbhlan agam
  Is ùbhlan uile aig càch,
Is ann tha m' ubhal cùbhraidh grinn
  Is cùl a chinn ri làr.

Ged tha mnathan chàich aig baile
  'Nan laighe is 'nan cadal sàmh,
Is ann bhios mise aig bruaich mo leapa
  A' bualadh mo dhà làimh.

Is mór a b'annsa bhith aig Griogair
  Air feadh coille is fraoich,
Na bhith aig Baran crìon na Dalach
  An taigh cloiche is aoil.

Is mór a b'annsa bhith aig Griogair
  Cur a' chruidh do'n ghleann,
Na bhith aig Baran crìon na Dalach
  Ag òl air fìon is air leann.

Is mór a b'annsa bhith aig Griogair
  Fo bharta ruibeach ròin,
Na bhith aig Baran crìon na Dalach
  A' giùlan sìoda is sròil.

Ged a bhiodh ann cur is cathadh
  Is latha nan seachd sìon,
Gheibheadh Griogair dhòmh-sa cragan
  'S an caidlimid fo dhìon.

  Ba hu, ba hu, àsrain bhig,
    Chan 'eil thu fhathast ach tlàth:
  Is eagal leam nach tig an latha
    Gun dìol thu t'athair gu bràth.

ANONYMOUS

It is a pity that I was not in the form of a sky-lark,
    With the strength of Gregor in my hands:
The highest stone in the castle
    Would be the stone nearest the ground.

And although I am without apples
    And all the others have apples,
There is my fragrant, handsome apple
    And the back of his head on the ground.

Although everyone's women are at home
    Lying quietly asleep,
It is I who am at the edge of my bed
    Beating my two hands together.

I'd rather be with Gregor
    On an extent of wood and heather,
Than to be with the petty Baron of Dall
    In a house of stone and lime.

I'd rather be with Gregor
    Sending the cattle to the glen,
Than to be with the petty Baron of Dall
    Drinking wine and ale.

I'd rather be with Gregor
    Under a rough hair-cloth coverlet,
Than to be with the petty Baron of Dall
    Wearing silk and satin.

Although there might be falling and drifting snow
    On the day the seven trumpets sound,
Gregor would find me a little rock
    In which we would sleep sheltered.

Ba hu, ba hu, little wanderer
    You are still but tender:
And I am scared that the day will not come
    That you will ever avenge your father.

1. August 1st.
2. For a full discussion of the blood-drinking motif, see Derick S. Thomson "The Blood-Drinking Motif in Scottish Gaelic Tradition"
    in *Indogermanica et Caucasica: Festschrift fur Karl Horst Schmidt zum 65*. Geburtstag. Eds. Roland Bielmeier and Reinhard Stempel.
    Walter de Gruyter (Berlin and New York) 1994. pp. 415-424

translated from Scottish Gaelic by
C. M. SHIPMAN

Sur ces entrefaits, Koch nous parle du pays (crincrin martial)

H. n'est pas les meules
N'est pas petit lanceur de pierre avec chambre réduite
N'est pas trente mille hommes de dépôt ou de recrues
N'est pas veuglaire
N'est pas Dampf Kraft Wagen
Pas unités mobiles de tueries
Pas propergol
Pas pas de l'oie
N'est pas ratissage nocturne
Pas colonne
N'est pas infiltration
Pas en Russie nous avions très souvent livré des corps à corps
Pas pistolet de bord
N'est pas piste Hô-Chi-Minh
H. n'est pas Hawker Fury
N'est pas bombarde
N'est pas Trommelfeuer
H. n'est pas dirigeable à carcasse rigide
Pas Shankill
Pas Hiwiss
Pas on-dé, on-dé demi-touuuuuuuuur gauche
N'est pas Huey Cobra, Long Tom, vagues d'assaut
N'est pas tromblon, clairon, opérateur
Pas un cloaque de dix centimètres avec du sang, des vers et de la merde
H. n'est pas la bombe
Pas coup de main
N'est pas cheddite
N'est pas Nobel et décibels
Nacht und Nubel
Pas du tout fourragère
N'est pas camp retranché
N'est pas pont aérien
Pas les renforts
N'est pas la course
Pas unités de consolation
N'est pas marche de flanc en vue de l'ennemi
N'est pas corvée de bois
H. n'est pas l'artillerie française

(continued)

Then Koch reported on the state of the country (ol' martial tune)

H. is not grindstones
Is not a small stone thrower with a small chamber
Is not 30,000 railway workers or recruits
Is not a heavy cannon
Is not Dampf Kraft Wagen
Not mobile units of slaughter
Not rocket propellant
No goose step
No night search
No marching column
Is not infiltration
Not in Russia where we often fought hand to hand
No gun on board
Is not the Ho Chi Minh Trail
H. is no Hawker Fury
Is not bombardment
Is not Trommelfeuer
H. is not a rigid-frame dirigible
No Shankill
No Hiwis
Not about, about-faaaaaaaaaace, left
Is not Huey Cobra, Long Tom, waves of attack
Is not blunderbuss, bugle, operator
Not a 10-centimeter latrine filled with blood, worms, and shit
H. is not the bomb
No help
Is not an explosive
Is not Nobel and decibel
Nacht und Nubel
Not at all shoulder lanyard
Is not an entrenched camp
Is not an airlift
Not the reinforcements
Is not the footrace
No civilian consolation units
Is not a flank unit marching at the sight of the enemy
Is no kindling duty
H. is not the French artillery

(continued)

159

Pas Stars and Stripes

Pas Nembutal

Pas fusil à aiguille

H. n'est pas le Bois-Bourru

N'est pas mon colonel, votre conduite mérite qu'on vous frappe dans le dos à coup de
  crosse

Pas Gurkhas

Pas le pitaine

Pas les ratas

Pas H des os pas H des guerres

N'est pas les munitions, les vivres et les arrières

Pas la ligne Morice

N'est pas les partisans

Pas soldat-laboureur

Pas l'ennemi avait déjà fait quelques tentatives pour passer

Pas grenadiers du roy

H. n'est pas De Havilland Mosquito

H. n'est pas la chaux

N'est pas les fours à chaux

Pas Totenkoff

Pas Ikara

N'est pas mégatonnage

Banja-Luka

Pas fusil boucanier

N'est pas transports de troupes

Pas les balles traçantes

N'est pas le gros des forces

Pas coffre à explosif

Pas aux arrêts

Pas aux aguets

N'est pas radome

Pas quadrillage

H. n'est pas la position, l'opération, le déploiement

N'est pas derrière les lignes

Pas les détachements

Pas il avait placé la majeure partie de sa cavalerie à l'aile droite

N'est pas Hotchkiss

Pas les ondes de choc

N'est pas la viande

Pas trop du calme dans les rangs

H. n'est pas la Distant Early Warning Line

N'est pas fusil de salve

Pas marsouin

Pas jumelles

Pas la Corée

Pas la Crimée

Pas Monowitz

(continued)

Not Stars and Stripes
Not Nembutal
No needle-gun
H. is not the Bois-Bourru
Is not my colonel, for your behavior you should be lashed with the butts of rifles
No Gurkhas
Not the cap'n
Not the grub
Not H-bones not H-wars
Is not ammunition, supplies, and the rear guard
Not the Morice line
Is not the partisans
Not peasant-soldier
Not the enemy who had already made a few attempts to go through
No royal grenadiers
H. is not De Havilland Mosquito
H. is not lime
Is not lime kilns
Not Totenkopf
Not Ikara
Is not megatons
Banja Luka
Not a buccaneer rifle
Is not the transport of troops
Not tracer bullets
Not the main body of troops
Not a case of explosives
Not under arrest
Not on the lookout
Not a radar shed
No occupation
H. is not the position, the operation, the deployment
Is not behind the lines
Not the detachments
Not he had stationed the bulk of his cavalry on the right flank
Is not Hotchkiss
Is not the shock waves
Is not the flesh
Not really silence in the ranks
H. is not the Distant Early Warning Line
Is not a salvo of artillery
No marine
No binoculars
Not Korea
Not Crimea
Not Monowitz

(continued)

Pas le Kemmel
H. n'est pas un vigoureux sabreur
Pas allons-y
N'est pas mes hommes
N'est pas l'amour pas la guerre
Pas couleuvrine
Pas le Kemmel
Pas un cloaque de dix centimètres avec du sang, des vers et de la merde
N'est pas mousquet à mèche
Pas Grand Quartier Général
H. n'est pas treillis, rangers et casque lourd
Pas cette odeur
Pas camouflage
N'est pas les barbelés
H. n'est pas fléau d'arme
N'est pas soldats je suis content de vous
N'est pas pertuisane à soleil
Pas Oberleutnant
Pas lésion cérébrale
N'est pas le fusil Krag
Take care ! n'est pas les gaz
Pas division blindée
Pas les 220 volts
Pas flanelle de l'enfant
Pas trop les viandes
Un peu camp retranché
N'est pas V2 Schneider
Pas la cervelle
Pas Kropatschek
N'est pas boîte à cristaux
Pas l'histoire des cloaques avec sang, vers et merde
H. n'est pas cosaques
Take care ! pas chiens de mer pas chiens de guerre
N'est pas Grodek
Pas banquettes de tirailleurs
N'est pas petit-matin-carrière-échappement-moteur
Take care ! n'est pas les gaz
H. pas le gaz
N'est pas le doigt sur la gachette
N'est pas Hanoï
Pas la Crimée
Pas planquez-vous, nom de Dieu!
N'est pas les meules
Pas la râte éclatée
H. n'est pas prise de guerre
Take care ! butin de guerre

(continued)

Not the Kemmel trenches
H. is not a hearty swordsman
Not let's go
Is not my men
Is not love not war
Not an old cannon
Not the Kemmel trenches
Not a 10-centimeter latrine filled with blood, worms, and shit
Is not a fuse musket
Is not General Headquarters
H. is not fatigues, combat boots, and helmet
Not this smell
Not camouflage
Is not barbed wire
H. is not flail
Is not soldiers I am proud of you
Is not halberd in the sunlight
Is not Oberleutnant
Not a brain lesion
Is not the Krag rifle
Take care! Is not the gas
Not armored division
Not the 220 volts
Not the child's flannel
Not really the flesh
A little entrenched camp
Is not V2 Schneider
Not the brains
Not Kropatschek
Is not a crystal radio
Not the story of the latrines filled with blood, worms, and shit
H. is not Cossacks
Take care! Not dogs of sea not dogs of war
Is not Grodek
Not ranks of infantrymen
Is not in-the-early-hours-quarry-exhaust-engine
Take care! Is not the gas
H. not the gas
Is not the finger on the trigger
Is not Hanoï
Not Crimea
Not dive, for god's sake!
Is not grindstones
Not the spleen burst
H. is not war spoils
Take care! War booty

(continued)

N'est pas la nuit
N'est pas la nuit n'est pas la guerre
N'est pas le gaz n'est pas les bières
Pas la gégène
Putain de guerre
Pas la gehenne
Paquet de nerfs
H. pas les fours
N'est pas la guerre
H. pas les faux
N'est pas la nuit
Pas Desfourneaux
N'est pas la guerre
H. pas la chaux

(l'imbécile de Koch)

JEAN-MICHEL ESPITALLIER

Is not the night
Is not the night is not the war
Is not the gas is not the caskets
Not the electrodes
Fucking war
Not Gehenna
Knot of nerves
H. not the crematory furnace
Is not the war
H. not the scythes
Is not the night
Not Desfourneaux
Is not the war
H. not lime

(stupid Koch)

translated from French by
OLIVIER BROSSARD & LISA LUBASCH

Das Paradies

Stufen flach wie die Zehen. Ungegängelt
Wehst du hinan in zedernzartes Grün.
Luft, um sie sachte durch den Leib zu ziehn.
Fresstempelchen. Jedoch es wird gedrängelt.

VOLKER BRAUN

Paradise

Doorsteps as even as toes. Unharnessed
You drift upward into the cedar-tender green.
Air, softly blowing through the body.
Temple of gluttony. Constantly nagging.

translated from German by
CECILIA ROHRER & MATTHEW ROHRER

Die Zickzackbrücke

Die bösen Geister laufen nur gradaus.
Als wie der Dämon
Der Ideologen
Mir nicht folgt in den blühenden Garten.

VOLKER BRAUN

The Zig Zag Bridge

The evil spirits only run straight ahead
As if the fiend
The idealist
Didn't follow me into the flowering garden

translated from German by
CECILIA ROHRER & MATTHEW ROHRER

Der Maurer von der Stalinallee

Unter den Großblöcken
Stoße ich auf einen Maurer. Er gehört
Zu der versunkenen Klasse
Die genaue Wände machte und
Den Aufstand. Im Traum
Führe ich ihn wieder auf das Gerüst
Schweißßgebadet
Eines Anfangs.

VOLKER BRAUN

The Wall at Stalin Avenue

Under the huge boulders
I stumbled upon a wall. It belongs
to the lost ranks
which created precision divisions and
the Revolution. In dreams
I lead him onto the scaffolding again
dripping with sweat.
A fine beginning.

translated from German by
CECILIA ROHRER & MATTHEW ROHRER

Düello

Yenilirsem yenilirim, ne çıkar yenilmekten?
Seninle çarpışmak kişiliğimi pekiştirir benim.
Ayak bileklerime kadar bu deredeyim işte,
Yerin yassı taşları tabanımın altında,
Alnımda birleşmekte güneşin raylarından
Hışırtıyla geçen kartalların sesleri.
Unuttuğum bir bitkinin yaprakları gibi
Göğsüme değerse kurşunların, ne çıkar?

Bilmem nişancılığı, tabanca kullanmadım;
Ama karşıma alıp seni horoz düşürmek de,
Seni vuramamak da yüreğimi pekiştirir benim.
Ölürsem güzel ölü olurum,
Saçlarıma yuva kurar bir anda kirpiler,
Kar, örtemeye kalkışır gökkuşağını,
Ve onurlu, yoksul böceklerin gazetecisi
Ben gülümserken resmimi çeker.

ÜLKÜ TAMER

The Duel

If I am defeated, I am defeated, what does it matter?
Dueling you will strengthen my character.
Here I am standing in this valley up to my ankles
The flat rocks of this ground are under the soles of my feet,
The shrieks of the eagles traversing the sun's rails
With a grating noise blend into my forehead.
If your bullets hit my chest like the leaves of a plant
I have long forgotten about, what does it matter?

I know nothing about marksmanship, I've never used a revolver;
But once I face you, both dropping the cock
And failing to shoot you will harden my heart.
If I die I shall make an attractive corpse,
In a split second, hedgehogs will make their nests in my hair,
The snow will endeavor to shroud the rainbow
And the journalist of the dignified poverty-stricken bugs
Will take snapshots of my smiling.

translated from Turkish by
TALAT HALMAN

L'attaque de la montagne

C'est peu de chose que de tordre un cou, d'en tordre dix, d'arracher du plancher une vieille fille geignarde avec le siège qu'elle y occupe, le faisant si précipitamment qu'elle s'écrase le crâne contre un meuble cependant que le fauteuil y perd un pied. Pour cela, la moindre colère, pourvu qu'elle soit vraie, suffit, mais attraper une montagne devant soi dans les Alpes, oser l'attraper avec force pour la secouer, ne fût-ce qu'un instant, la grandiose ennuyeuse qu'on avait depuis un mois devant soi. Voilà qui mesure ou plutôt démesure l'homme.

Mais pour cela il faut une colère-colère. Une qui ne laisse pas une cellule inoccupée (une distraction même infime étant catégoriquement impossible), une colère qui ne peut plus, qui ne pourrait plus reculer (et elles reculent presque toutes quoiqu'on dise quand le morceau est démesurément gros).

Ce me sera donc tout de même arrivé une fois. Oh je n'avais pas à ce moment-là de griefs contre cette montagne, sauf sa sempiternelle présence qui m'obsédait depuis deux mois. Mais je profitai de l'immense puissance que mettait à ma disposition une colère venue d'une lance portée contre ma fierté. Ma colère en son plein épanouissement, en son climax, rencontra cette grosse gêneuse de montagne, qui irritant ma fureur, l'immensifiant, me jeta, transporté, impavide, sur la montagne comme sur une masse qui sôi pu réellement en trembler.

Trembla-t-elle? En tout cas, je la saisis.

Attaque presque impensable, à froid.

C'est mon summum d'offensive jusqu'à présent.

HENRI MICHAUX

Attacking the mountain

It's not much, to twist someone's neck, or ten, to snatch up from the floor a whiny old maid, along with the chair she's sitting on, so hastily that her head is crushed against some piece of furniture and the chair loses its footing. All it takes is the slightest anger, provided it's authentic, but to grab a mountain in front of you in the Alps, daring to grab it hard enough to shake it, if only for an instant, that grandiose bore you'd been looking at for a whole month. That's what gives a man his true measure or rather goes beyond it.

But for that you need to be angry-angry. Not one cell of your body can be left out of it (you can't afford even the slightest distraction), an anger incapable of retreating (and almost all of them retreat, whatever people say, when the thing's too big to swallow).

All the same, it did happen to me once. Oh, it's not that I had any objection to that particular mountain, except for its never-ceasing presence which had been obsessing me for two months. But I took advantage of the immense power that I had available thanks to my anger from an injury to my pride. My anger in its full splendor, at its peak, encountered that hugely irritating mountain, enormously magnifying my rage, hurled me, undaunted, upon the mountain as if it could really have been shaken.

Was it? In any case, I grabbed it.

Usually, almost unthinkable.

It's my most successful endeavor up to now.

translated from French by
MARY ANN CAWS & PATRICIA TERRY

Alphabet

Tandis que j'étais dans le froid des approches de la mort, je regardai comme pour la dernière fois les êtres, profondément.

Au contact mortel de ce regard de glace, tout ce qui n'était pas essentiel disparut.

Cependant je les fouaillais, voulant retenir d'eux quelque chose que même le Mort ne pût desserrer.

Ils s'amenuisèrent et se trouvèrent enfin réduits à une sorte d'alphabet, mais à un alphabet qui eût pu servir dans l'autre monde, *dans n'importe quel monde.*

Par là, je me soulageai de la peur qu'on ne m'arrachât tout entier l'univers où j'avais vécu.

Raffermi par cette prise, je le contemplais invaincu, quand le sang avec la satisfaction, revenant dans mes artérioles et mes veines, lentement je regrimpai le versant ouvert de la vie.

HENRI MICHAUX

Alphabet

While I was in the chill of approaching death, I looked at people, as if for the last time, deeply.

At the deadly contact of this icy look, all but the essential disappeared.

Nevertheless I searched them, wanting to preserve something that even Death couldn't take from their grasp.

They diminished in size, until finally they shrank to a sort of alphabet, but an alphabet which could have been useful in the other world, *in any other world.*

I had rid myself of the fear that the whole universe in which I'd lived would be torn from me.

So strengthened, I was contemplating this triumph, when my relief sent the blood back into my arteries and my veins, and I slowly climbed back up the open slope of life.

translated from French by
MARY ANN CAWS & PATRICIA TERRY

Sahir Ludhyanvi's "Taj Mahal"

TTaj Mahal" created an enormous sensation among poetry enthu-
siasts in the Indian Subcontinent when it was first published
in a magazine. The poem attracted so much attention because it
viewed the most famous and esteemed monumnet of that region
in a new anddifferent light.

The author used the pen name Sahir Ludhyanvi. His real name was Abdul Haiy
(1921–1980) and he wrote in Urdu, the musical language widely spoken in Pakistan
and India. Born in the Punjab, Sahir came of age before World War II when the re-
gion was shaking off British rule and when Taraqqi Pasand Tahreek (the Progressive
Movement) was mobilizing many young people. Like many writers of his time, Sahir
often has a political message in his work. His poems are also appreciated for their
emotional force and musicality. "Taj Mahal" typifies all of these qualities.

Sahir's enormous popularity as a poet in the Urdu-speaking world rests on only
two books—*Bitterness*, a collection of short poems that contains "Taj Mahal"; and
Shadows Speak, a longer appeal for peace.

After Pakistan and India became independent Sahir used his skills as a poet to become a highly successful song writer in the Bombay film industry, and published his lyrics in the volume *The Singing Troubadour*. He fought for higher wages for lyricists and went on to become the president of the labor union that represents film workers.

The musical qualities of "Taj Mahal" can only be suggested in translation. Urdu poetry relies on syncopated accents and repeated sounds that add a rhythmic and vocal intensity almost unknown in contemporary English-language poetry.

One interesting sidebar is that the poem inspired a famous couplet that rebutted Sahir's view of the Taj Mahal, parodying Sahir's own phrasing in the concluding lines. Instead of Sahir's lines:

A shah wielded his gold
To mock the tenderness of the poor like us

the response was:

A poet wielded his bitterness
To mock a living monument of love

HAMIDA BANU CHOPRA, ZACK ROGOW, & NASREEN G. CHOPRA

تاج محل

تاج، تیرے لیے اک مظہرِ الفت ہی سہی
تجھ کو اس وادیِ رنگیں سے عقیدت ہی سہی
میری محبوب! کہیں اور ملا کر مجھ سے

بزمِ شاہی میں غریبوں کا گزر کیا معنی؟
ثبت جس راہ پہ ہوں سطوتِ شاہی کے نشاں
اس پہ الفت بھری روحوں کا سفر کیا معنی؟

میری محبوب! پسِ پردۂ تشہیرِ وفا
تو نے سطوت کے نشانوں کو تو دیکھا ہوتا
مردہ شاہوں کے مقابر سے بہلنے والی
اپنے تاریک مکانوں کو تو دیکھا ہوتا

ان گنت لوگوں نے دنیا میں محبت کی ہے
کون کہتا ہے کہ صادق نہ تھے جذبے ان کے
لیکن ان کے لیے تشہیر کا سامان نہیں
کیونکہ وہ لوگ بھی اپنی ہی طرح مفلس تھے

یہ عمارات و مقابر، یہ فصیلیں، یہ حصار
مطلق الحکم شہنشاہوں کی عظمت کے ستوں
دامنِ دہر پہ اس رنگ کی گلکاری ہیں
جس میں شامل ہے ترے اور مرے اجداد کا خوں

میری محبوب! انہیں بھی تو محبت ہوگی
جن کی صناعی نے بخشی ہے اسے شکلِ جمیل
ان کے پیاروں کے مقابر رہے بے نام و نمود
آج تک ان پہ جلائی نہ کسی نے قندیل

یہ چمن زار، یہ جمنا کا کنارہ، یہ محل
یہ منقش درو دیوار، یہ محراب، یہ طاق
اک شہنشاہ نے دولت کا سہارا لے کر
ہم غریبوں کی محبت کا اڑایا ہے مذاق
میری محبوب! کہیں اور ملا کر مجھ سے

••

SAHIR LUDHYANVI

Taj Mahal

The Taj may symbolize love to you
But even if you revere this valley running with colors
Meet me somewhere else my love

Do the poor like us belong
At this royal gathering
On these paths etched with the "majesty" of royalty
What could our love-filled souls amount to

My love
I wish you had looked
Behind this curtain of devotion
And seen the haughtiness there
Amused by this emperors' mausoleum
You're losing sight of our own dark houses

Countless people have fallen in love
Who dares call their feelings false
But like us they lacked the wealth to display them

This fortress these tombs
This façade and these ramparts—
The azimuth of the shah's limitless power—
Are woven with colors
But soaked in the blood of our ancestors

Didn't they also love—
The ones who crafted this beauty—
The tombs of their sweethearts
Go unmarked unnoticed
No one ever lit a candle for them

With these parks and gardens this riverbank of the Jamuna this palace
These inlaid portals and spandrels arches and niches
A shah wielded his gold
To mock the tenderness of the poor like us
My love
Meet me somewhere else

translated from Urdu by
HAMIDA BANU CHOPRA, ZACK ROGOW, & NASREEN G. CHOPRA

Cây Na

Cây na bên cửa phòng tôi
Hiền xinh như thể nụ cười trẻ thơ
Buổi hoàng hôn sớm tinh mơ
Cây na dáng đứng như chờ đợi ai
Lá vô tư, rễ miệt mài
Búp non đẹp tựa tình ai buổi đầu
Hoa nở bé thấy gì đâu
Bỗng kia trái đã nhú mầu tơ non
Lá xanh ôm ấp quả tròn
Dịu dàng như mẹ ấp con tháng ngày
Quả xanh lẫn với màu cây
Thoáng nhìn nào có ai hay biết gì
Giữa trời nghe tháng năm đi
Trăm mắt na mở nói gì với tôi
Cây na đứng lặng thế thôi
Lặng im mà nói bao lời sâu xa.

LÂM THỊ MỸ DẠ

Custard Apple Tree

By my door the custard apple tree
Is like a child smiling, charming
From early dawn to early evening
The tree stands, like someone waiting

The strong roots, the carefree leaves
Buds like stirrings of first love
Blossoms so small I can scarcely see
And then the fruit, its raw-silk color

The fruit is warmed by green leaves
Like an unborn child by its mother
Green fruit blends with green tree
So a quick glance reveals nothing

I feel the time passing by outside
Then a hundred apple-eyes speak
The tree just stands there silent, silent
With words that are countless and deep

translated from Vietnamese by
MARTHA COLLINS & THUY DINH

ללא כותרת

הֲרֵי הֵם בְּמֶרְכַּז חַיַּי
שְׁתֵּי יַלְדוּת גֶּבֶר אִשָּׁה

וְלָמָּה אֶפְחַד
לְכָל דָּבָר רַק אַרְבַּע פִּנּוֹת

גְּדוּשַׁת כַּוָּנוֹת אֲנִי מְחַיֶּכֶת
כִּמְעַט מַגִּישָׁה פְּרָחִים
חוֹשֶׁבֶת לְטַאטֵא אֶת הֶעָפָר שֶׁנֶּעֱרַם

אֲבָל הִיא יוֹדַעַת עָלַי הַכֹּל
לָכֵן הִיא צוֹרַחַת בְּקוֹל מְטוֹס מוּסְטוֹט

מֵעֵבֶר לַקִּיר הַיְלָדוֹת בְּגַרְבַּיִם
שְׁמוּטִים הֵן פַּרְפָּרִים חֲלָקִים
קַלּוֹת כִּמְאֻשָּׁרוֹת

וְהַסַּבְתָּא עוֹרֵב מִנַּבֵּא מִמַּעֲבֵה הָאָרֶן
מִדּוֹר לְדוֹר לְדוֹר

NURIT ZARHI

untitled

For they are at the center of my life,
two girls, a man, a woman.

Why should I be afraid,
each thing has only four corners.

Full of intents I smile
almost proffer flowers
plan to sweep the accumulating dust.

But she knows everything about me
and so screeches with the sound of shifting beds.

Beyond the wall the girls in drooping socks
are smooth butterflies
light as if happy.

And grandma-crow divines in the thicket of the pine
from generation to generation to generation.

translated from Hebrew by
TSIPI KELLER

de Sección I de **Negro marfil**

El arpa en su lluvia diagonal simetría de las partes la patria en lluvia

derrumbes volcán abierto erupción   lo ácido en la córnea

en una lámpara votiva el deseo está emplazado

from Section I of **Ivory Black**

The harp in its diagonal rain symmetry of its parts homeland in the rain

landslides volcano open eruption   what is acid in the cornea

in a votive light desire is set in place

(continued)

Allí estaba sin estar el país acueducto estaba sin hablarme y era claro

en su querer estar a solas   Me dijeron que por su boca hablaría una

sola vez Era una lengua marcada por cisuras   Gráficamente tenía una

cruz enmedio era un grabado en líquido abrasivo   Una grasa dorada

penetra de arriba hacia los lados allí donde debieran ir los brazos

pero no hablaba sufría el país con un voto de silencio y descalzado

(continued)

There it was without being there the aqueduct country was there without

speaking to me and it was clear in its desire to be there alone   They

told me that with its mouth it would speak just once   It was a tongue

marked by incisions   Graphically it had a cross at the middle it was

an engraving in liquid abrasive   A golden oil penetrates from above

reaching the sides there where the arms should be but it was not

speaking the country was suffering with a vow of silence and barefoot

(continued)

La morera asoma frutos negros

Pájaros cerrados   Inconclusos

Pequeña semilla   Atada

Con juncias   Como el corazón

En la mano: Ofrenda

Cabe el adiós agradecido

El índice señala lo alto

El umbral   Del cielo   Oculto

Soluble   En fuga   Pájaro

Sobre blancos   Abierto ya

              En resurrección

MYRIAM MOSCONA

The white mulberry puts out black fruits

Closed birds   Inconclusive

Small seed   Bound

With sedges   Like a heart

In the hand: Offering

The grateful good-bye goes here

The index points to the height

The threshold   Of the sky   Hidden

Soluble   Escaping   Bird

Atop whites   Open now

            In resurrection

translated from Spanish by
JEN HOFER

Cuvette

Raturée dans une petite cour
de câble difforme.
Glycine dans la penée joie.
Le dessin et sa danse
marque la durée entre les rideaux.
Rien d'impur.
Tes flammes sculptent les miroirs
dans la lumière sous la Terre.
Au dedans un foyer transmission
de réglage au bol vermillion
mange des concombres.
Boire donne le visage jeunesse.
Dans ma chair c'est la vie de cheveux.
Les animaux recontrent la solitude de vis
à l'heure arabesque dans les clefs.
La résidence béante et tordue
des clovisses
Tout à coup comme un juge hermétique
occupe où donc
un homme couché à plat ventre.

FRANCIS PICABIA

A Watch Cap

Scratched out in a small courtyard
of misshapen cable.
Glycine in the thought happiness.
The drawing and its dance
mark the duration between the curtains.
Nothing impure.
Your flames sculpt the mirrors
in the light under the Earth.
Within a hallway transmission
of the tuning to the vermilion bowl
eats cucumbers.
Drinking makes the face youthful.
In my flesh there is the life of hairs.
The animals meet the solitude of screws
On time arabesque in the keys.
The open pit of a household twisted
by cockles
All at once as a hermetic judge
is busy where then
a man lying flat on his belly.

translated from French by
JEFFREY JULLICH

código de barra

solos o en compañía todos los príncipes se fueron
quedamos los de siempre los de otras veces los que ya
nos conocemos voy a ser breve te propongo

un lugar apartado mirar las últimas estrellas
tomar juntos el primer café con leche del domingo
nada más puedo ofrecerte sólo tengo lo que soy

además de un erre cinco con asientos abatibles

GARCÍA CASADO

bar code

one by one or all together the crown princes fled
only the regulars were left those that were here before
we know each other well enough i'll make it quick i propose

a distant place watching the last stars die out
sipping the first coffee together on sunday morning
i can't offer you anything else i only have what i am

an r and a 5 and a few folding chairs

translated from Spanish by
CHRIS MICHALSKI

uso

el techo es el mismo la mancha
gris la misma el mismo sonido
de los muelles cuerpo anónimo

cosa-por-detrás cierra los ojos
ábrete cariño el mismo tacto
que otros anónimo duro mecánico

directo al centro sin apenas rubor
sin reparo al modo al encaje a la duda
el uso el mismo uso cariño venga

date la vuelta sólo tres golpes uno
gemido dos cerrar los ojos tres gritar
gritar no sentir nada nada

GARCÍA CASADO

use

the floor is the same the gray
stain the same the same sounds
of the harbor anonymous body

thing-left-behind close your eyes
open love the same sense
as everyone else anonymous hard mechanical

direct to the center with barely a blush
without a thought for manners for lace with no doubts
the use the same use love come on

turn around just three hits one
groan two close your eyes three scream
scream don't feel anything anything

translated from Spanish by
CHRIS MICHALSKI

la edad del automóvil (reprise)

año dos mil quince la que será tu mujer
despliega los planos del sexto izquierda
número veinte calle poeta jaime gil de biedma

tres dormitorios cocinados cuartos de baño
estás aquí en el mismo lugar donde siempre
estuviste muy lejos quedan ahora las afueras

y son otros vientres los que buscan su refugio
lejos de aquí del mismo lugar donde hace tiempo
tú también descubriste la edad del automóvil

GARCÍA CASADO

age of the automobile (reprise)

year two thousand fifteen the woman that'll be your wife
unfolds the plan of the sixth-floor apartment
number twenty jaime gil de biedma avenue

three bedrooms kitchen two baths
you're here the same place you've always
been now the suburbs are unbelievably far away

other wombs now seek his refuge
far from here the same place where you yourself
once discovered the age of the automobile

translated from Spanish by
CHRIS MICHALSKI

Mirno

tako miren sem. luna je rdeča. ravnokar je prilebdela
izza oblakov. počasi kot radoveden, kobacav otrok.
na televiziji je majhna pisana vaza s posušeno vrtnico
in nasilje. morijo se s puškami in rokami. vse gre
zelo na hitro in kot da je zares. monika tega ne ve.
ona tiho spi. spi in diha enakomerno kot mašina.
noč je. vendar slišim, da avtomobili ne spijo.
tudi mačke ne. vrešče se preganjajo pod našim oknom.
niti jaz ne spim. sedim in ne morem reči, da razmišljam,
samo opazujem žilo, ki ti liže dlan kot reka.

TONE ŠKRJANEC

Calm

I am so calm. red moon. it has just come drifting
from beyond the clouds. slowly, like an inquisitive toddler.
on television there is a small florid vase with a dried-up rose
and violence. killings with hands and guns. it's all
very fast, as though it were for real. monika doesn't know this.
she sleeps quietly. sleeps and breathes evenly like a machine.
it is night. but I can hear the cars not sleeping.
nor cats. screeching, they chase each other beneath our window.
I'm not asleep either. I sit, can't say I'm thinking, just
watching the vein that licks your palm like a river.

translated from Slovenian by
ANA JELNIKAR

Kale

nič nisem rekel, niti besede. kar sedel sem,
roke sklenil za glavo in poletel. zarezal sem
skozi mehkobo in naprej v tišino. duša me boli
ker mi pušča. iz nje kaplja kot iz pipe v kuhinji.
kapljice se potem na tleh objamejo okoli ramen
poljubljajo se in hihitajo, da nastane luža,
ki se pretvarja, da je morje. pogledam se vanj
in iz oči mi poletita dva beloglava orla. iz druge smeri
dežuje pesem klavirja. vsem lažejo. tudi ribam.
prinesel sem ti kale in štrucko s sirom.

TONE ŠKRJANEC

Calla Lilies

I said nothing, not a word. I just sat there,
put my arms behind my neck and took off flying. I cut through
the softness and further into the silence. my soul hurts
because it leaks. it drips like the kitchen tap.
the drops, putting their arms around each other,
kiss and giggle until a puddle forms,
which pretends to be a sea. I look at myself in it
and out of my eyes two white-headed eagles come flying. from the other direction
a piano piece comes pouring. they lie to everyone. to fish as well.
I brought you Calla Lilies and a roll with cheese.

translated from Slovenian by
ANA JELNIKAR

L'Invetriata

La sera fumosa d'estate
Dall'alta invetriata mesce chiarori nell'ombra
E mi lascia nel cuore un suggello ardente.
Ma chi ha (sul terrazzo sul fiume si accende una lampada) chi ha
A la Madonnina del Ponte chi è chi è che ha acceso la lampada?—c'è
Nella stanza un odor di putredine: c'è
Nella stanza una piaga rossa languente.
Le stelle sono bottoni di madreperla e la sera si veste di velluto:
E tremola la sera fatua: è fatua la sera e tremola me c'è
Nel cuore della sera c'è,
Sempre una piaga rossa languente.

DINO CAMPANA

Slit

—after Campana

All summer, oversexed as if a supernova
And the sky too romantic to suggest, in star-light, the other world
Enough to cause our hearts a leaving.
But who has (in a second story bedroom window, lamplight wilts) who has
To the virgin of uncrossings who is who is she who has luck enough to fuck?—there's
This season which must be one of decay: there's
In this life, some sufferings as crimson and fallen, vibrant as autumn's tremblings.
The stars are spinsters' buttons, the night strangling as sex:
And it's all silly, all this flicker and wavering and our ghosts given over and there's
In the cleave of evening there's
Always one red plague languishing.

translated from Italian by
JENNY BOULLY

Un homme et une femme absolument blancs

Tout au fond de l'ombrelle je vois les prostituées merveilleuses
Leur robe un peu passée du côté du réverbère couleur des bois
Elles prominent avec elles un grand morceau de papier mural
Comme on ne peut en contempler sans serrement de coeur aux anciens étages d'une
    maison en démolition
Ou encore un coquille de marbre blanc tombée d'une cheminée
Ou encore un filet de ces chaînes que derrière elles se brouillent dans les miroirs
Le grand instinct de la combustion s'empare des rues où elles se tiennent
Comme des fleurs grilles
Le yeux au loin soulevant un vent de Pierre
Tandis qu'elles s'abîment immobiles au center du tourbillon
Rien n'égale pour moi le sens de leur pensée inappliquée
La fraîcheur du ruisseau dans lequel leurs bottines trempent l'ombre de leur bec
La réalité de ces poignées de foin coupe dans lesquelles elles disparaissent
Je vois leurs seins qui mettent une pointe de soleil dans la nuit profonde
Et donc le temps de s'abaisser et de s'élever est la seule mesure exacte de la vie
Je vois leurs seins qui sont des étoiles sur des vagues
Leurs seins dans lesquels pleure à jamais l'invisible lait bleu

ANDRÉ BRETON

A Man and a Woman Absolutely White

In the parasol's depths I see the marvelous prostitutes
Their dresses faded under streetlamps the color of the woods
They take a huge fragment of wallpaper out with them for a walk
A fragment you cannot look at without heartache over the demolition of ancient floors
Or worse over the white marble shells fallen from mantels
Or worse over a filament of their necklaces blurring in the mirrors behind them
A powerful instinct for combustion seizes the streets where they wait
Like singed flowers
Their eyes raising a wind of stone in the distance
While they remain engulfed and motionless at the whirlpool's center
For me nothing can equal the significance of their careless thoughts
Or the fresh gutter water in which their little boots steep the shadows of their beaks
Or the reality of those fistfuls of hay into which they disappear
I see their breasts put a dot of sun into the deep night
The time they take to lie down and to get up is the only exact measure of life
I see their breasts which are stars over the waves
Their breasts in which the invisible blue milk sobs forever

translated from French by
CLAYTON ESHLEMAN

La impaciencia

Los poetas construyen torres de Babel; los filósofos, murallas de China.

Todas las sumas evocan al cero.

Protesto porque estoy convencido, no para convencer.

El rasgo más notable del europeo es la impaciencia: ella nos hace creer que las catedrales góticas son antiguas.

ANGEL CRESPO

Impatience

Poets build Towers of Babel; philosophers, Great Walls of China.

All sums evoke the zero.

I protest because I'm convinced, not because I'm trying to convince.

Impatience is the European's most notable trait: it makes us believe that gothic cathedrals are ancient.

translated from Spanish by
STEVEN J. STEWART

Renunciaciones

Quien lo recuerda todo no puede aprender.

El olvido nos obliga a inventar, a descubrir lo que ignorábamos.

Prefiero el atardecer: soy occidental.

Algunos poetas parecen ignorar a la décima musa: la que aconseja no escribir.

ANGEL CRESPO

Renunciations

One who remembers everything cannot learn.

Forgetting obliges us to invent, to discover what it was we didn't know.

I prefer twilight: I'm occidental.

Some poets seem to ignore the tenth muse: the one who says to not write.

translated from Spanish by
STEVEN J. STEWART

XXXI

PAENE insularum, Sirmio, insularumque
ocelle, quascumque in liquentibus stagnis
marique uasto fert uterque Neptunus,
quam te libenter quamque laetus inuiso,
uix mi ipse credens Thuniam atque Bithunos
liquisse campos et uidere te in tuto.
o quid solutis est beatius curis,
cum mens onus reponit, ac peregrino
labore fessi uenimus larem ad nostrum,
desideratoque acquiescimus lecto?
hoc est quod unum est pro laboribus tantis.
salue, o uenusta Sirmio, atque ero gaude
gaudente, uosque, o Lydiae lacus undae,
ridete quidquid est domi cachinnorum.

CATULLUS

31

Little eye of islands and almost-islands,
Sirmio, whatever both Neptunes bring
on the inland waters or the enormous sea,
how glad I am when I look upon you,
scarcely believing that I've left Thynia
and Bithynian fields to see you safely.
O what is better than the end of anxiety
when the mind sets its troubles aside
and we return home, weary from travel,
to relax in the beds we missed so much.
This alone makes everything worthwhile.
Hello, lovely Sirmio! Enjoy your master's
joy, and you, o lake of Lydian waves,
laugh whatever laughter is in the house.

translated from Latin by
RICK SNYDER

XXXII

AMABO, mea dulcis Ipsitilla,
meae deliciae, mei lepores,
iube ad te ueniam meridiatum.
et si iusseris, illud adiuuato,
ne quis liminis obseret tabellam,
neu tibi lubeat foras abire,
sed domi maneas paresque nobis
nouem continuas fututiones.
uerum si quid ages, statim iubeto:
nam pransus iaceo et satur supinus
pertundo tunicamque palliumque.

CATULLUS

32

Please, my sweet Ipsitilla,
my darling, my sunshine—
invite me over this afternoon,
and when you do, make sure
that your door's not bolted
and that you don't step out—
but stay at home and prepare
for nine straight fuckulations.
If you have any plans, call me
immediately: I'm lying down
after a big lunch, boring holes
through my cloak and tunic.

translated from Latin by
RICK SNYDER

XLVIII

MELLITOS oculos tuos, Iuuenti,
si quis me sinat usque basiare,
usque ad milia basiem trecenta
nec numquam uidear satur futurus,
non si densior aridis aristis
sit nostrae seges osculationis.

CATULLUS

48

Your honey-sweet eyes, Juventius—
if they'd let me keep kissing them
I'd keep kissing them three hundred
thousand times—and I'd never seem
close to satisfied, even if the crops
of our kissings were packed tighter
than the dried-out ears themselves.

translated from Latin by
RICK SNYDER

海岸

シャム双生児の仔やぎは
月足らずで生まれた
私たちは頭のくっつきあった二匹を引きちぎり
一方は焚火の上の野菜スープの鍋に放り込み
もう一方は母やぎの胎内へともどしたが
通ってきた産道をもう一度くぐらせるために
母やぎの体に差し込んだ角笛の先から
まだ湯気のたった仔やぎを滑らせねばならなかった
こうした作業はすべて
遠くに山影がかすむ草原でおこなわれた

ヒトの場合それは
晩秋の海岸の浜小屋でおこなわれる
小屋の前に据えられた調理台の上に
両膝を折って仰臥する妊婦は
ふたたび方の胎児を迎え入れたのち
月満ちるまでのときを小屋に閉じ籠って過ごし
やがて投網の袋床に子を産み落とすと
初雪の日に海岸を立ち去って
二度と
この土地に近づくことはない

ABE HINAKO

Seashore

The Siamese-twin kids
were born prematurely.
We tore apart the two that were joined at the top of their heads,
threw one of them into a vegetable-soup pot on a bonfire
and took the other back into the she-goat's womb,
but in order to make it go through the uterus once again
we had to force the still-steaming kid to slide
into the horn inserted into the she-goat's body.
All this work was carried out
on a plain with mountains hazy in the distance.

In the case of a human
it is carried out in a beach hut on the seashore in late fall.
The pregnant woman who lies supine, knees bent,
on the cooking table set up before the hut
once again welcomes back one of the fetuses,
passes the time confined in the hut, until the moon becomes full,
gives birth to a child on the bed of a casting net,
walks away from the shore on the day of the first snow,
and never
approaches the area again.

translated from Japanese by
HIROAKI SATO

De ciel et de tungstène

L'aérodrome évince le dieu terme au bout de la pelouse
L'hôtesse a plus de mille fois plus fait plus de miles
Que mille fois tous les conquistadors
        Qui s'en vanterait
Le promenoir des anges pour y songer

        Un mariage sur les ailes
        On est monté penser aux Chutes:
        Volcan au cours inverse volcan
Cônerie d'eau, ta pointe d'ultra-sons vers le bas
Sucette pour Hadès, abreuvoir des touristes niagarés

        L'hydre avion au rugir égal
Qui rompt d'un coup l'arctique avec cent hommes à dos...
Adieu Hercule! La terre embrassée formidable,
        Cessons de dire mal du métal
        Du voisin homme de la terre

Oiseaux de bonheur au ciel porte-voie
Oiseaux pris à partie (pour le tout)
Vous incitez à vous suivre de bec
Ailés qui vous hélez par les valvules d'air
Au cœur de l'an qui fait battre les glaces
        Vous nous mâchez les mots

MICHEL DEGUY

from Tombeau de Du Bellay © *Editions Gallimard, Paris, 1973*

Of Sky and of Tungsten

The aerodrome evinces the term-god at the far end of the grounds
The stewardess has more than a thousand times more gone more miles
Than a thousand times all the conquistadors
        Who would boast of it
The angels' promenade to ponder it

        A marriage upon the wings
        We went up to think of the Falls:
        Volcano flowing backwards volcano
Conoid water vulva, your tip of ultra-sounds downward
Sucker for Hades, trough of niagarated tourists

        Airplane hydra of the steady roar
Which breaks through to the arctic at one go with a hundred men astride . . .
Farewell Hercules! The tremendous earth embraced,
        Let's stop speaking ill of metal
        Of our neighbor man of the earth

Birds of happiness in the route-carrier heavens
Birds taken to task apart (for the whole)
You prompt with beak to follow you
Winged ones who hail one another near the air nozzles
In the heart of the year rattling the panes
        You mince words with us

translated from French by
WILSON BALDRIDGE

Antée

L'être sans attachement que nous sommes
Descend maintenant les marches sans se retourner
(Sur le Tage à Versailles au Latran)
Silhouette du mortel qui fut riche en crises
Mais il n'est plus herculéen   s'usant
Sur un rythme trop lent pour s'en aviser
S'identifie plutôt moderne aux victimes
La mort cerne cet Antée qu'elle hante
Et qui déjà ne touche plus que d'un orteil à la terre dérobée

MICHEL DEGUY

from Jumelages *suivi de* Made in USA © *Editions du Seuil, Paris, 1978*

Antaeus

The being without attachment whom we are
Now goes down the stairs without looking back
(On the Tagus at Versailles in the Lateran)
Silhouette of the mortal once rich in crises
But he's no longer Herculean   wearing himself out
At a pace too slow to notice
Rather modern identifies with victims
Death surrounds this Antaeus whom it haunts
And who no longer touches but with a single toe the subsiding earth

translated from French by
WILSON BALDRIDGE

Karıma Mektup

33-11-11, Bursa, Hapishane

Bir tanem!
Son mektubunda:
"Başım sızlıyor
      yüreğim sersem!"
           diyorsun
"Seni asarlarsa
      seni kaybedersem;"
           diyorsun;
"yaşıyamam!"

Yaşarsın karıcığım,
kara bir duman gibi dağılır hatıram rüzgârda;
yaşarsın, kalbimin kızıl saçlı bacısı
en fazla bir yıl sürer
      yirminci asırlılarda
         ölüm acısı.
Ölüm
bir ipte sallanan bir ölü.
Bu ölüme bir türlü
      razı olmuyor gönlüm.
Fakat
emin ol ki sevgili;
zavallı bir çingenenin
      kıllı, siyah bir örümceğe benzeyen eli
         geçirecekse eğer
         ipi boğazıma,
mavi gözlerimde korkuyu görmek için
      boşuna bakacaklar
         Nâzıma!
Ben,
alaca karanlığında son sabahımın
dostlarımı ve seni göreceğim,
ve yalnız
yarı kalmış bir şarkının acısını
      toprağa götüreceğim...

(continued)

Letter to My Wife

November 11, 1933, Bursa Prison

My one and only!
You say
        in your last letter:
"I have a splitting headache.
            my heart is bewildered."

You say:
        "If they hang you,
            if I lose you
                I cannot live!"

You can live, my dear wife;
like black smoke, my memory will fade in the wind.
You will live, my heart's red-haired woman:
in the twentieth century
            mourning the dead
                    lasts no more than a year.

Death...
    a corpse swinging from a rope,
I just can't resign my heart
        to a death like that.

But rest assured, my love,
            if the hairy hand of a poor gypsy,
                like a black spider,
                    will slip a rope
                        around my neck,
they will look in vain
        into the blue eyes of Nazim
                    to see fear!

In the twilight of my last morning,
I
    will see my friends and you,
and I will only take
        into the pit
            the sorrow of an unfinished song.

(continued)

Karım benim!
İyi yürekli,
altın renkli,
gözleri baldan tatlı arım benim;
ne diye yazdım sana
                istendiğini idamımın,
daha dâva ilk adımında
ve bir şalgam gibi koparmıyorlar
                        kellesini adamın.
Haydi bunlara boş ver.
Bunlar uzak bir ihtimal.
Paran varsa eğer
        bana fanile bir don al,
tuttu bacağımın siyatik ağrısı.
Ve unutma ki
daima iyi şeyler düşünmeli
                bir mahpusun karısı.

NAZIM HİKMET

My wife!
My good-hearted,
golden bee
     with eyes sweeter than honey!
Why did I write you
         they asked for a death sentence?
The trial has just started
and they don't pluck a man's head
            like a turnip.

Never mind, forget all this.
These are not likely at all.
If you have money,
     buy me flannel underpants:
I got sciatica pains in my leg again.
And don't forget,
A prisoner's wife
     should always have good thoughts.

translated from Turkish by
TALAT HALMAN

Der Winkel von Hahrdt

Hinunter sinket der Wald,
Und Knospen ähnlich, hängen
Einwärts die Blätter, denen
Blüht unten auf ein Grund,
Nicht gar unmündig
Da nemlich ist Ulrich
Gegangen; oft sinnt, über den Fußtritt,
Ein groß Schiksaal
Bereit, an übrigem Orte.

FRIEDRICH HÖLDERLIN

Recess

The forest dips and the leaves
hang in like loose buttons

The ground comes out to meet them
mouthing, Ulrich went here

Here is where big things to come
find a left-over spot and a footprint

translated from German by
SAM STARK

Nouvelle-Orléans

Tout d'un coup,
le ciment armé et la tuyauterie de fer
ne poussent plus.
Rues étroites, gondolées,
avec des bouquinistes comme sur les quais,
où on trouve la littérature française de La Harpe, dépareillée,
verdie par la moisissure des tropiques.
Derrière les jalousies
il y a de vieilles dames à camées qui croient que la dernière guerre
c'est la guerre de Sécession,
et que *thesedamnedyankees* s'écrit en un seul mot.
Elles n'ont jamais dépassé la rue du Rempart.
Leurs négresses à cheveux blancs lisent Volney et vous disent en français: «Soyez assis».
Tous ces gens sont ruinés
et organisent des bals.
Ils furent Américains pour échapper à la France jacobine.
Mais ils se disent aussi Français pour ennuyer les Américains.
Ce sont les seules personnes aux États-Unis qui emploient le mot: détester.
Aussitôt après Canal St.
ce scandale cesse
et nous rentrons dans la ville américaine.

PAUL MORAND

from Poèmes © *Editions Gallimard, Paris, 1973*

New Orleans

Suddenly
the reinforced concrete and iron pipe
stop growing.
Narrow twisted streets
and second-hand bookstalls line the quays
where you find La Harpe's study of French literature, set incomplete,
green with tropical mildew.
Behind the shutters
there are old ladies wearing cameos who think that the last war
was the War of Secession,
and that "thesedamnedyankees" is written as one word.
They've never gone further than Rempart Street.
Their white-haired Negro women read Volney and tell you in French, "Be seated."
All these people are bankrupt
and organize fancy-dress balls.
They become American to escape Jacobin France.
But they also say that they're French to irritate the Americans.
They're the only people in the United States who use the word "detest."
Right after Canal Street this scandal stops
and we re-enter the American city.

translated from French by
RON PADGETT & BILL ZAVATSKY

Désert Mohave

Neige sur le désert. Cristallerie des fontaines.
Sur l'infini, jusque sur le ciel,
des chevaux et des Ford en liberté.
Une voie ferrée. Perspective pointue des 2 rails
se rejoignant, par ennui, dans un paysage extrêmement abstrait.
Végétation de barbelés.
Salons en troncs d'arbre. Poêle. Chaleur d'isba.
Aux murs des peaux de lion-de-montagne et d'ours.
Par terre, des tapis indiens, losanges blancs, svastikas rouges.
Des jarres de paille avec dessins noirs,
où se reconnaît la manière des Indiens Hopi.
Des hommes entrent, poussés par l'envie de déjeuner, les pieds pleins de boue
    rouge,
feutre, Far-West, cabossé, gants blancs, cigare. Pas rasés.
Une jeune fille, trop habillée, souliers vernis, met les assiettes.
Le père, en salopette à bretelles, change un pneu.
Personne ne parle plus.
Assis dans le fauteuil d'honneur,
fait de bois d'élans,
je lis dans le journal d'*El Paso*, à haute voix, et à la demande générale,
la liste des récompenses offertes
pour les criminels à arrêter.

PAUL MORAND

Mohave Desert

Snow on the desert. Crystalware from the springs.
Horses and Fords running loose
to infinity, right up to the sky.
A railroad track. Pointy perspective of the two rails
meeting, out of boredom, in the most abstract of landscapes.
Barbed wire vegetation.
Tree-trunk drawing rooms. Stove. *Isba* heat.
On the walls, skins of bear and mountain lion.
On the floor, Indian rugs, white diamond patterns, red swastikas.
Straw baskets with black designs
in which you recognize the Hopi Indian style.
Some men come in, ready for a big breakfast, their feet covered with red clay,
battered western-style hats, white gloves, cigars. Unshaven.
A young girl, over-dressed, shoes shined, sets the table.
Her father, in overalls, changes a tire.
The conversation stops.
Sitting in the best armchair
made of elk horns,
I read aloud from the El Paso newspaper, by popular request,
the list of rewards offered
for criminals on the most-wanted list.

translated from French by
RON PADGETT & BILL ZAVATSKY

Landskaber

I

At.
At gå.
At gå baglæns i egne fodspor.
Skridt: Navn.
Gang: Bevægelige navne.
Du spurgte mig, om jeg havde lyst til at gå en tur,
    og spørgsmålet
forgrenede sig ud i landskabet.
Landskabet prøver sin stemme på os,
    det prøver at udtale
vores fremmedartede navne,
men vi er heller ikke i stand til
at formulere dét. Hvad vil du vide?
Det siger: „Vær ikke bange, bliv her."
    Vi siger: „Vi er her allerede."
Æbletræerne blomstrer selvindlysende
og lærer os at se med ord.

II

Det andet landskab.
    Om igen: Ord er døre, der står på klem.
Du havde en blomstrende æblegren med til mig.
Undertiden tager svalerne
fejl og flyver omkring inde i huset.
Dette leben. Gæsterne ringer og fortæller,
    at de er på vej.
Vi går tur i svalernes perspektiv. I deres øjne
er vi belyste gåder.
De kommenterer os højlydt:
„Ma, come si fa?" Svaler går ikke på jorden.
De manøvrerer i luften. Bjerge og træer står stille.
    Jeg bevæger mig
i forhold til dem. En figur på en grund
uden bagside. Svalerne kliner mine øjne
    til med vådt ler
og virkelige billeder.

(continued)

Landscapes

I

To.
To walk.
To walk backwards in one's tracks.
Step: Name.
Walk: Movable names.
You asked me if I felt like going for a walk,
    and the question
branched out into the landscape.
The landscape tries out a voice on us.
    It tries to pronounce
our unfamiliar names,
but we are also unable
to formulate it. What do you want to know?
It says: "Don't be afraid. Stay."
    We say: "We are already here."
The apple-trees blossom self-evidently
and teach us to see with words.

II

The second landscape.
    Again: Words are doors that are ajar.
You had a blossoming apple-branch with you for me.
At times the swallows make a
mistake and fly around inside the house.
This bustle. Guests phone to say
    they are on their way.
We go for a walk from a swallow's eye view. In their eyes
we are lit-up enigmas.
They make clamorous comments about us:
"Ma, come si fa?" The swallows do not walk on the ground.
They manoeuvre in the air. The mountains and trees stand still,
    I move
in relation to them. A figure on a background
with no reverse. The swallows daub my eyes
    shut with wet clay
and real images.

(continued)

III

Gæsterne er kommet.
Man kan ikke undgå at se
en forrykt gud give sig til kende
i deres blikke, når de banker på døren
        og taler ophidset
sammen i mobiltelefon.
Så vil de hentes på fjerntliggende stationer,
men når jeg sætter deres kufferter frem,
vil de ikke vide af dem, og deres gaver er ikke
        pakket ind.
Vi blev vækket midt på natten
af et skybrud. Landskabet læste os
        som en åben bog. Bagefter duftede
alting af varm jord og vådt græs, men vi var for
generte til at lægge betydning i det.

IV

At sige: Alting. Det samme som at sige: Gå.
At sige: Gå. Det samme som at sige: Lad
        landskabet gå gennem dig. At sige: Landskab.
Det samme som at sige: Alting. Gå baglæns,
det er malerens gestus, og straks
poserer landskabet, som om det var det,
        der skulle males, og ikke
Mona Lisa, la Gioconda.
Landskabet trækker i os som et barn, der keder sig,
det holdes kun oppe af cikadernes horisontdrone.
Træd ind i huset. Træd ind gennem rammen.
        Det samme som at sige: Træd ind i landskabet.
Jeg samler alt-hvad-jeg-ved i små stakke
og stikker dem i brand.

V

Døden skriver og skriver.
I dag kom et talende oliventræ hen til mig og sagde:
„Livet er en overgang fra ingenting til
        ingenting."
Men sådan noget kan man da ikke
sige til nogen? Landskabet folder sig ud som
siderne i en bog. Ein Nervenreiz. Un état d'âme.
        Vi har ingenting forstået. Sådan er dét.
Det som står mellem landskabets linjer
lader sig ikke læse. Vi folder punktummerne

(continued)

III

The guests have arrived.
One cannot help seeing
a demented god revealing himself
in their looks when they knock on the door
        and talk excitedly
with each other on their mobile phones.
They want to be fetched at distant stations,
but when I bring out their suitcases,
they want nothing to do with them, and their gifts haven't
        been wrapped.
We were woken in the middle of the night
by a cloudburst. The landscape read us
        like an open book. Afterwards everything
smelled of warm earth and wet grass, but we were too
shy to attribute any meaning to that.

IV

To say: Everything. The same thing as saying: Walk.
To say: Walk. The same thing as saying: Let
        the landscape walk through you. To say: Landscape.
The same thing as saying: Everything. Walk backwards,
that is the gesture of the painter, and immediately
the landscape poses, as if it were
        about to be painted, and not the
Mona Lisa, la Gioconda.
The landscape tugs at us like a child that is bored,
it is only held up by the horizon drones of the cicadas.
Step into the house. Step in through the frame.
        The same thing as saying: Step into the landscape.
I collect everything-I-know in small stacks
and set them on fire.

V

Death writes and writes.
Today the talking olive tree came over to me and said:
"Life is a transition from nothing to
        nothing."
But you can't say something like that
to anybody? The landscape unfolds outwards like
the pages of a book. Ein Nervenreiz. Un état d'âme.
        We have understood nothing. And that's that.
What's between the lines of the landscape
is impossible to read. We unfurl the full stops   (continued)

ud til stjerner, og gæsterne kommer tilbage
fra aftenturen med paniske øjne og tøjet
plettet af vin.

VI

Landskabet i huset: Det regner.
　　Men det regner ikke. Det meste er sandt.
Gæsterne vil have morgenmad på sengen.
Midt i det rasende græs.
Myrerne transporterer
landskaber af vidt forskellig oprindelse
　　rundt imellem sig.
Myrerne lægger dem i en bunke,
　　og landskaberne bliver ét.
Udvis den største forsigtighed i omgang med
landskaber. Kontinenterne vandrer. Vi elsker
　　som nysgerrige børn, og æbletræerne
har tabt deres blomster.

VII

Hold nu op! Disse trapper af kød
der giver efter for hvert skridt
　　og fører lige op i teoretiske overbygninger om økonomi
og døde forfatteres seksualitet.
Det knirker i den stupide analyse.
　　Der er jo kun at sige,
at tilfældet konkurrerer med døden
om at komme først til de nyfødtes hjerner.
Jeg er ufuldendt, en krank af stålkugler,
der rasler ud over marmorgulvet, gæsternes stemmer
　　invaderer mig og bla bla bla

VIII

At. Dette: At.
Man kan ikke sige: „Gå til venstre ved det store træ,"
for sætningen når ikke helt derhen.
Nu vil gæsterne have natmad. De skændes om
　　hvem, der skal sove hvor.
Blikket løber og løber, det strækker ud, det farer frem
og tilbage over samme uforståelige linje.
Men landskabet er ulæseligt,
　　og vi kaster
knogleskygge. Kom, lad os gå en tur i stedet.
Vi går gennem døre af en vis størrelse.

(continued)

into stars, and the guests return from
their evening walk with panic-stricken eyes and their clothes
spattered with wine.

VI

The landscape inside the house. It's raining.
   But it's not raining. Most things are true.
The guests want to have breakfast in bed.
In the midst of the living grass.
The ants transport
landscapes of widely differing origins
     round amongst themselves.
The ants place them in a heap
     and the landscapes become one.
Display the utmost caution when dealing with
landscapes. The continents migrate. We make love
     like curious children, and the apple trees
have lost their blossom.

VII

Oh lay off! These stairs of flesh
that give way at each step
     and lead directly up into theoretical superstructures on economy
and the sexuality of dead authors.
The stupid analysis creaks somewhat.
     All it amounts to is saying
that chance is competing with death
to arrive first at the brains of the new-born.
I am unfinished, a crank of steel bearings
that rattle across the marble floor, the guests' voices
     invade me and blah blah blah

VIII

To. This: To.
One cannot say: "Turn left at the big tree",
for the sentence does not quite reach it.
Now the guests want a late snack. They are arguing about
     who is to sleep where.
The gaze runs and runs, stretches out, dashes back
and forth across the same incomprehensible line.
But the landscape is unreadable,
     and we cast
skeletal shadows. Come, let's go for a walk instead.
We walk through doors of a certain size.

(continued)

Dørene lukkes og åbnes. Læs: Dørenes størrelse
   er afstemt efter menneskenes.
I landskabet er dørene beregnet til guder.

IX

13. december: Santa Lucia-dag.
Vi leder en kvinde ind i kirken, hun bærer
sine øjne frem på et lille fad.
   Men miraklernes tid er forbi.
Inde ved siden af står en meteorolog
i sin gummicelle af et tv-studie
og lover godt vejr de næste par uger.
Vi blander os ikke,
   det føles bare pinligt
med alle de valutakurser og computergrafik.
Hvert digt lyser sit stykke af verden op med sin lygte.
Det er en måde at præcisere den på.
   Kære
Vi er to synkrone ure,
der går med hvert sit liv.
Vi skiftes til at bære hinanden
som trætte børn. Til sidst falder vi til ord,
   skriver videre på hvert sit kødbrev til vinden.
Med mine fingerspidser forsikrede jeg mig om,
   at du alligevel giver mening.
Kærligst

X

Jeg oversatte det, du havde sagt,
men udelod det væsentligste.
Kom, vi forvandler os til træer!
Gro. Sæt blade og nye skud.
Svalerne glider
   gennem havens luft
som lydløse skalpeller.
Ildfluerne syer himlen sammen med lysende sting.
Landskabet stiller nærgående spørgsmål.
Men vi kan ikke få et ord frem, sætningerne
   kroger sig som gamle træer:
Det vigtigste må vi holde for os selv.

(continued)

The doors shut and open. Read: The size of the doors
        is determined by that of the humans.
In the landscape the doors are designed for gods.

IX

13 December: St Lucia's Day.
We lead a woman into the church, she is bearing
her eyes on a small platter.
        But the age of miracles is past.
Inside close by stands a meteorologist
in his rubber cell of a TV studio
promising good weather for the next couple of weeks.
We do not interfere,
        it feels simply embarrassing
with all the stock exchange figures and computer graphics.
Each poem lights up its piece of the world with its torch.
It is a way of making it precise.
        Dear,
We are two synchronous watches,
going with our separate lives.
We take turns carrying each other
like tired children. Finally we fall into words,
        continue our separate flesh-letters to the wind.
With my finger tips I made sure
        that you make sense even so.
Love,

X

I translated what you had said,
but left out the
most important thing.
Come, let's change into trees!
Grow. Put out new leaves and shoots.
The swallows glide
        through the garden air
like soundless scalpels.
The fireflies sew the sky together with shining stitches.
The landscape put indiscreet questions.
But we cannot utter a word, the sentences
        grow gnarled like old trees:
We have to keep the most important thing to ourselves.

(continued)

XI

Månen over dalen, på flugt.
Vi tør ikke sove, så klart som den brænder.
    Landskabet flytter ind. Det leder efter noget
spiseligt. Gæsterne kommer: Jeg troede, det var dig.
Gæsterne tager af sted: Det var dig.
    Det er os, der er gæster, indvandrere
der bliver ved med at gå. Gik vi bare lidt mere
realistisk til værks, var vi allerede fremme.
    Vinstokkenes grønne jakkesæt
blafrer på skråningerne.
    Se hellere den anden vej,
for husene går omkring ude på vejene, de har
forladt deres fundamenter. Opbrud overalt.
Stederne invaderer os, og forsvarsløse lader vi os
    føre ingen vegne. Vi kunne slå os ned her: Vi.

XII

Man prøver igen med den desperate mund,

men det kan ikke lade sig gøre. Måske
er det ordene,
    som siger os.
Gå videre. Svalerne knevrer.
Opmærksomheden indfanget
af det tilsyneladende uvedkommende:
    Her har alle adgang.
Gæsterne går i ét med udsigten.
De knepper. Og æbletræerne har andet for.
Jeg forlader mig selv som et hus:
    Jeglandskabet.
Undskyld. Det var ikke det, jeg mente.
Det skulle have været anderledes.
    Mere oprigtigt. Men det var umuligt.

(continued)

XI

The moon above the valley, in flight.
We do not dare sleep, it is burning so brightly.
     The landscape moves in. It is looking for something
edible. The guests arrive: I thought it was you.
The guests leave: It was you.
     It is us, there are guests, immigrants
that keep on walking. If we only got down to it
a little more realistically, we would already be there.
     The green lounge suit of the vines
flutters on the hillsides.
     Better look the other way,
for the houses are out and about on the roads, they have
left their foundations. Departures everywhere.
The places invade us, and defenceless we allow ourselves
     to be led nowhere. We could settle here. We.

XII

One tries again with a desperate mouth,

but it cannot be done. Perhaps
it is the words
     that say us.
Move on. The swallows chatter.
Attention caught
by what is apparently irrelevant:
     Here everyone has access.
The guests merge with the view.
They screw. And the apple trees have other business.
I leave myself like a house:
     The I-landscape.
Sorry. That wasn't what I meant.
It ought to have been different.
More honest. But that was impossible.

(continued)

XIII

Forfra. Betragt hver ting.
Jeg ved godt, at landskabet prøver at forestille
sig os med de store fugleskræmsler
øverst på bakken. Den blinde kat
    jager i den hemmelige have
Fugleskræmsler, bakker, træer, solsikkemarker
kommer helt tæt på og gransker vores ansigter.
Men landskabet ligger uden for enhver betydning.
Det tænker sit. På den anden side:
    Vi er træer med ben.
Vi kan ikke blive her. Kom lad os gå.
Lad os gå tanken ud.

XIV

På grund af min meget ringe orienteringsevne
    er jeg gået forkert, men når alt kommer til alt,
er det ganske underordnet. Om lidt går jeg
„der" hen. Før var jeg „her". Lige nu er jeg et sted
    mellem „der" og „her".
Myrerne slæber landskabet væk,
sukkerkorn mellem arbejdende kæber,
stump for stump. Men myrerne selv er stumper
forbundet af en enorm association.
    Se ikke sådan på mig! Jeg prøver jo bare
at sige tingene lige ud. Råbemanden råber „Scirocco",
og fint sand fra Sahara dækker alle overflader.

XV

Om igen: Det var ikke sådan, det skulle være.
Send mere ultramarin, for landskabet er
størknet støj. Der er så meget andet, der skal
siges, før det er for sent.
Det fortsætter bare,
    det vokser frem
som græs og mug på alle overflader.
Vedbendhænder rækkes ind over en mur.
Forårets maskine kører af sig selv.
Vinden suser i oliventræerne. En støj af ingenting.
Har vi forsømt nogen mulighed?
    Lad os spise af de grimme knogletallerkner i aften.
Jeg satte en skål mælk ud til den blinde kat.
Verden faldt fra hinanden og blev sat sammen igen
    af det intelligente barn.

(continued)

XIII

As you were! Consider each thing.
I'm well aware that the landscape tries to imagine
us with the big scarecrows
on the hilltop. The blind cat
    stalks in the secret garden.
Scarecrows, hills, trees, fields of sunflowers
come up close and scrutinise our faces.
But the landscape lies beyond every meaning.
It thinks its own thoughts. On the other hand:
    We are trees with legs.
We cannot stay here. Come, let's walk.
Let's walk the thought-plank.

XIV

Due to my poor sense of direction
    I have got lost. But, all things considered,
that's of minor importance. In a moment I will walk
"over there". Before, I was "here". Right now I am a place
    between "there" and "here".
The ants lug off the landscape,
grains of sugar between working mandibles,
bit by bit. But the ants themselves are bits
linked by an enormous association.
    Don't look at me like that! I'm only trying
to say things straight as they are. The Shouter shouts "Sirocco",
and fine sand from the Sahara covers every surface.

XV

Once again: That was not the way it was meant to be.
Send me more ultramarine, for the landscape is
congealed noise. There is so much else that has to
be said before it is too late.
It just keeps on,
    it grows
like grass and mould on each and every surface.
Ivy hands are handed in across a wall.
Spring's machine is self-operating.
The wind sighs in the olive trees. A noise of nothing.
Have we neglected some opportunity?
    Let's eat off the ugly white bone plates tonight.
I put out a bowl of milk for the blind cat.
The world fell apart and was put together again
    by the intelligent child.

(continued)

XVI

En vildt oplyst færge ude af kontrol
    pløjer gennem landskabet.
Jeg vidste ikke, at den havde ligget på dok
inde i huset, men det er nytårsaften,
og gæsterne har kappet fortøjningerne.
    Giv slip! Vi er flygtninge, der hænger over rælingen
på tilfældets båd. Fortsæt,
for der er ikke andet end digte
    og rodet hverdag at sætte mod tidens
ondskab og svimlende groove.
Jeg siger: Jeg elsker hvert bedøvende slag
    fra dit hjerte. Du siger: Det er, som om jeg
var dig. Men du skal ikke være bange.
    Det er du jo, og digtet står
og skratter som en gammel transistor
inde i tusmørkets kaos.

XVII

Ord: Deres antal forøges, når jeg bruger dem.
Svalerne flyver omkring med dem i munden.
    De hænger i græsset, de klæber til brændenælderne.
Det vi er: Et gråt pulver rørt op i skyerne.
Det vi ikke er: Landskab. Dette mere: Til siden, til siden.
    Det fortsætter uden for rammen. En sang
nogen bliver ved at nynne.
Vi bevæger os fra højre mod venstre. Spejlskrift.
Gæsterne råber på kaffe og sender e-mails.
Deres stemmer fylder huset ud. Om natten lejer
    kaos sig ind i det forseglede værelse.
Om dagen sover flagermus fra digtets tag.
    Jeg går ned for at hugge brænde. Øksen sidder
klar i huggeblokken.

XVIII

Fra den anden side af landskabet høres en hund,
der uopfordret bekræfter, at verden eksisterer.
    En motorsav. Stemmer. En klokke. Svalerne.
En sølvedderkop løber frem og tilbage og
trækker alle konturer op. Der findes nattergale,
    der synger om dagen, vanvittige,
fordi de har
glemt at drømme. Slangerne parrer sig på
stierne. Solen bevæger sig ikke.

(continued)

XVI

A wildly lit ferry out of control
        ploughs through the landscape.
I did not know it had been docked
inside the house, but it is New Year's Eve,
and the guests have cut the moorings.
        Let go! We are refugees hanging over the railings
on the boat of chance. Keep going,
for there is nothing else than poems
        and a cluttered everyday to pit against
the evil and dizzying groove of time.
I say: I love each deadening beat
        of your heart. You say: It is as if I
was you. But you are not to be afraid.
        For you are, and the poem stands
laughing like an old transistor
into the chaos of twilight.

XVII

Words: Their number increases as I use them.
The swallows fly around with them in their beaks.
        They hang in the grass, they stick to the stinging nettles.
What we are: A grey powder mixed up with the clouds.
What we are not: Landscape. This more: Sideways, sideways.
        It continues beyond the frame. A song
someone keeps on humming.
We move from right to left. Mirror-writing.
The guests call for coffee and send e-mails.
Their voices fill the whole house. At night
chaos rents the sealed room.
During the day the bat sleeps from the roof of the poem.
        I go downstairs to chop firewood. The axe is
ready in the chopping-block.

XVIII

From the far side of the landscape a dog can be heard
confirming uninvited that the world exists.
        A motorsaw. Voices. A bell. The swallows.
A silver spider runs back and forth,
defining all the contours. There are nightingales
        that sing during the daytime, madly,
because they have
forgotten to dream. The snakes mate on
the paths. The sun does not move.

(continued)

Måske varer det ikke længe, før det hele
er forbi? Vi må fatte os i korthed,
prøve at få det hele med.
     I vores fravær åbner huset sin bog
og læser højt for sig selv.
Det er virkelig blevet aften, og tingene står frem
hver for sig, hellignøgterne og urørlige.

XIX

„Den anden side af landskabet," siger du.
Vil du gerne derhen? Drejer det sig om at slippe
     igennem, om at komme frem til noget?
Vi standser op her. Landskabet er for
selvfølgeligt til at være på kortet. Vi vil gerne
kunne rumme det, men det vender hele tiden
den mest indlysende side imod os.
     Nøglen: At gå.
Gæsterne låser sig inde på toilettet
og bruger alt det varme vand.
Men i dag betyder det ingenting. Vi kan være
     ligeglade. Vi smiler venligt og kommer ikke til
fornuft igen.

XX

Jeg lukker den blinde kat ind.
     Den har en muldvarp i munden.
Også muldvarpen har fem
fingre på hver hånd, en håndværker med
hård hud fra landskabets underside.
Gæsterne falder ned fra træerne
     og får hjernerystelse.
Aftenen kommer og lægger sig nervøst
rundt om os: Den har fået tændt mere lys,
end den selv kan nå at slukke.
     Et sted i landskabet drømmer det
om stjernefald og jordskælv.

XXI

Baglæns gennem tankegange, tingene lyser op
som grønne dioder. Opad fra kaffe på baren,
     huskede pludselig det fortegnede kort fra
skolens biologibog, hvor kroppen lå foldet ud
over hjernebarken: De store hænder, de store læber,
     tungen, struben, kønsdele, arme, øjne.

(continued)

Perhaps it will all be over,
shortly? We must needs be brief,
seek to include everything.
    In our absence the house opens its books
and reads aloud to itself.
It is really evening, and everything stands out
individually, sacred-sobering and sacrosanct.

XIX

"The other side of the landscape", you say.
Would you like to go there? Is it a question of squeezing
        through, of reaching something?
We stop here. The landscape is too
inevitable to be on the map. We would like to
be able to contain it, but it keeps on turning
the most obvious side in our direction.
    The key: To keep on walking.
The guests lock themselves in the toilet
and use all the hot water.
But today it doesn't matter. We needn't
        care less. We give a friendly smile and do not
come to our senses again.

XX

I let in the blind cat.
It has a mole in its mouth.
The mole also has five
fingers on each hand, a workman with
calluses from the underside of the landscape.
The guests fall from the trees
        and get concussed.
Evening comes and lies down nervously
around us: It has caused more lights to be lit
than it can manage to put out.
    Somewhere in the landscape it dreams
of falling stars and earthquakes.

XXI

Backwards through trains of thought, the things light up
like green diodes. Upwards from coffee at the bar
    the badly drawn map from the school biology book
suddenly remembered, where the body lay spread out
over the cerebral cortex: The big hands, the big lips,
        the tongue, the throat, genitals, arms, eyes.   *(continued)*

Vi er deforme kykloper, som strækker os
langlemmede mod en imaginær tvilling.
Videre. Opad i skråskrift.
Landskabet skriver og skriver.
        Nu: Tankerne udpumpet af skridtenes rytmiske
snorken. Så bagefter: Hvordan skal det gå?
Pengene smuldrer som gamle aviser. Videre.
Der ligger huset på bjerget i landskabet. Osv.
        En vidtåben mund midt i det aftalte.
Jeg går lige ind. I døren står min tvilling
        og rækker mig sin kæmpemæssige hånd.

XXII

Af en eller anden grund er jeg kommet ud til havet.
Hvad skal jeg her? Lindskib.
        Gæsterne siger: Landskabet er et hav.
Men det er det ikke. Det er: Ingenvegne.
Det trækker op til
storm. Jeg forlader havet og skyerne som det,
de er: Skitser til et landskab.
        Havet korrumperer.
Svalerne søger sammen i flokke. Også vi ville
gerne kunne flyve,
ikke sandt, Leonardo?
Men de flyvemaskiner vi opfinder, falder hele tiden ned.
        Jeg er ikke sikker i min sag. En gammel frakke.
Måske er det noget af mig selv, jeg har glemt i
distraktion? Noget grønt fra landskabet?
Der står en mand foran huset i en gammel frakke
        og hugger brænde. Det kunne have været mig.

(continued)

We are deformed cyclopes, stretching out
long-limbed towards an imaginary twin.
Keep going. Upwards in italics.
The landscape writes and writes.
  Now: Thoughts pumped out of the steps' rhythmic
snoring. And afterwards: How will it all turn out?
The money crumbles like old newspapers. Keep going.
There lies the house on the mountain in the landscape. Etc.
  A wide-open mouth in mid-agreement.
I walk straight in. My twin stands at the door,
  stretching out a gigantic hand.

XXII

For some reason I have come down to the seashore.
What am I doing here? Lindscipe.
  The guests say: The landscape is a sea.
But it is not so. It is: Nowhere.
A storm is
brewing. I leave the sea and the clouds as what
they are: Sketches of a landscape.
  The sea corrupts.
The swallows crowd together. We too
would like to be able to fly,
wouldn't we, Leonardo?
But the flying machines we invent keep falling down.
  I am not sure about this: An old coat.
Perhaps I've forgotten something of myself
absent-mindedly? Something green from the landscape?
There's a man in front of the house in an old coat,
  chopping wood. It could have been me.

(continued)

XXIII

Skal vi begynde?
Melder klar: Ordene blomstrer.
Men landskabet er blufærdigt,
    det synker så let under vægten af alle disse øjenpar.
Gæsterne ringer og siger tak for sidst.
Vi savner allerede deres muntre stemmer.
Træerne øverst på bakken bærer frugt.
    En arm rækker mig et æble. Der er faktisk
en hånd for enden af armen
og et æble i hånden, men armen selv
sidder ingen steder. Hånden vinker.
Dørene åbner sig: Svalerne flyver mod syd.
    Digtet er en vej, der går gennem landskabet.
Den drejer og drejer,
og det er den vej, jeg skal.

MORTEN SØNDERGAARD

XXIII

Shall we begin?
Clear announcement: The words blossom.
But the landscape is shy,
    it so easily sinks under the weight of all these pairs of eyes.
The guests phone and say thanks for a great evening.
We already miss their cheerful voices.
The trees at the top of the hill bear fruit.
    An arm reaches me an apple. There is actually
a hand at the end of the arm
and an apple in the hand, but the arm itself
is attached to nothing. The hand waves.
The doors open: The swallows fly southwards.
    The poem is a path through the landscape.
It turns and turns,
and it is that path I am to take.

translated from Danish by
JOHN IRONS

Homophonic Feature

EOIN BAS N-DEARG 'S A N-DRUIM R' A THAOIBH,
MAR DO CHUIM AN CEARD GO CÕIR
LUCHT 'GAR CHASMHAIL CLEASA CEOIL—
EOIN 'S A SLEASA D' ASNAIBH ÕIR.

These lines were translated based on their
sound to create the following poems:

Ian be ass and he are gas and rum, are a toad be he
Ma dock him and she are go choir
Look, tiger chase him hell, cross'a soil
Ian's a sleaze and ass and a boor.

ALAN B. ABRAMSON

○

Eoin, the bass player, would not dare to drum,
Nor would he get chummy with a go-go girl.

Light may make a chasm look like heaven,
But Eoin's only weakness is the love of gold.

BILLY COLLINS

○

When a passing beard, sand-drummer, thief . . .
Martyr him and see her go squiring
Lucky girl, handsome, hale (classic kill),
When she slays at day a knave in the weir.

SHARON DOLIN

○

Eonism's base Neanderthal darling drum-throbs *uh uh*
Sea do chew him and sears his gong-choir
Lucid gargle   "chasm-hail"   cleavage oil—
Eon sleaze doses the naibe-whore

CHRISTINE HUME

(Homophone into Yiddish)

אין באַסיין דער גאָס. אײן טרוימער אַ טויב
מער דאָ שום אָנצעאַרטיק. קאַיאָר
ליכטיקער חתימה. אײַל-קליעשטש אײל
און ס'אַ סליחות אָדעס-נײַ בחור.

○

(Transliteration)

In baseyn der gos. Eyn troymer a toyb
mer do shum onteartik. Kayor
likhtiker khsime. Ayl-klyeshtsh eyl
un s'a slikhes Odes-nay bokher.

○

(Translation)

In a pool the torrent. One dreamer, a dove
no more uninvolved. Dawn
on the bright seal. Quickly-clutched ale,
a pardon for the boy straight from Odessa.

FAITH JONES

○

from 'The Kosher Undine'

Under the indrumming, darkening moil,
the sea doe grazes the bristling ocean.
A light leap into the hail-clenching chasm
sparks from split hooves unbridlable vowels.

JOYELLE MCSWEENEY

He lights his drum aflame,
   Charges at the moon,
With stalks of wheat for a sword.
   The light is imperial
During the midnight sun—
   It drums on him,
Until in flames he runs
   Into the fields. In the heat,
He's no musician. Nor warrior.

RICK MOODY

O

Cars in the hills running to work
My pain's too hard; go sing
Luck's hardly abysmal. The mice clean your cell
The road wuz an awful place to knife that sailor.

EILEEN MYLES

O

Yawnface the shout of drumsong people
Ocean's will eat god's choir
Aurora chasing man opens earth with skymouth—
Yawnface of season's nevered fire.

EDWIN TORRES

Even bass 'n' drums and drummer Taoist—
marred chums and charred go-carts—
locked gauchos, hale cleats, ceased oil—
even so sleazy a dozen—nab air.

SUSAN WHEELER

○

Anyone has the urge and the dream to begin
to go and to do whatever water and dogs and skies want
Look light right through chamisoles if you want to—
Anyone's feeling sleepy in fresh perfume

○

One has dread and thumping and a handbook
The sea has made a mistake but that can be corrected
It would take too long to mix up all its letters
One would be inside a camel waiting to be born gold

○

You have no thoughts really and really are a thief
Smears you eat and there goes your heart
Fish with pimples are aggravated by your sun
You were asleep eons ago when tall warriors ate your heart

○

I was just small then and underneath nothing
more a chink somewhere an and a piece of a heart
someone needs someone to slather them with sunblock
I deny I'm a part of any of this

DARA WIER

The New Princeton Encyclopdia of Poetry and Poetics (eds. Alex Preminger and T. V. F. Brogan, Princeton Univ. Press, 1993, p. 178) translates this late Medieval Celtic stanza as:

Birds crimson-clawed are backed around its rim, so deftly crafted by the artist that they seem about to sing—birds whose shapes are ribbed with gold.

Contributors' notes

Poets

ABE HINAKO

"Born in Samarkand, Uzbek," she once said of her life, "I moved south through China during the Cultural Revolution and reached Japan toward the end of the 60's. I wrote my first book of poems, *Shokumin-shi no Chikei (Topography of a Colonial City)*, in 1989, to show how much I had achieved in my study of Japanese in the ensuing twenty years." Actually, Abe was born in Tokyo in 1953. Her third and most recent book, *Kaiyobi no Onna-tachi (Women on Seaday)*, in 2001, won the Takami Jun Prize.

CONSTANTIN ACOSMEI

Constantin Acosmei was born in Tîrgu Neamţ, Romania and now works as a librarian in Iaşi. "Male Dicat" first appeared in *Jucaria mortului (The Dead Man's Toy*, 1995), which won the *Asociaţiei Scriitorilor din Iaşi* (Writers' Association from Iaşi) prize for a first book of poetry.

AMARU

The Sanskrit *Amarusataka* is currently dated to the middle of the eighth century. Tradition ascribes the anthology to a single author, a King Amaru or Amaruka of Kashmir. Modern scholars have been divided as to whether Amaru wrote all the poems, whether he was a compiler, even whether he existed. The translations in this issue are from the Southern Indian edition of the *Amarusataka*, compiled by Vemabhupala in about 1400. It was edited by C. R. Devadhar and published under the title *Amarusatakam with Srngaradipika of Vemabhupala* by Motilal Banarsidass, Delhi, 1954.

CARLITO AZEVEDO

Carlito Azevedo was born in Rio de Janeiro in 1961. His five books of poetry include *Collapsus Linguae* (1991), which received the Prêmio Jabuti, and *Sublunar* (2001), an edition of his collected poems. He is the editor of the literary magazine *Inimigo Rumor*.

VOLKER BRAUN

Volker Braun is one of the foremost poets of the former East Germany, and though he was often at odds with the DDR's political system, he is a poet wary of the Western hegemony. His poetry was widely published in East and West Germany before unification, and in 2000 he won the prestigious Georg Büchner Prize. Braun is the author of many books of poetry, essays, fiction, and plays and is regarded as one of the most prominent living German poets.

ANDRÉ BRETON

Born in Tinchebray, France, André Breton (1896–1966) was a founder of the French Surrealist Movement. He is widely known for writing *The Manifestoes of Surrealism* and *Nadja*.

DINO CAMPANA

Dino Campana (1885–1932), in addition to being a poet whose style has been described as "hallucinatory," was also an escape artist, having escaped many times from both prison and an asylum. He was among the Futurists and Crepuscolari, and was known to have peddled his *Orphic Songs*.

GARCÍA CASADO

Born in Córdoba in 1972, García Casado's first book of poems *Las afueras (The Suburbs)* received El Ojo Crítico prize and was a finalist for the Spanish National Prize for Poetry. His work has been included in several anthologies. He has also been involved in the creation of the journals *Cinco*, *Reverso*, and *Recuento*.

CATULLUS

Gaius Valerius Catullus, scholars generally agree, lived from 84 BC to 54 BC. Most likely from a noble provincial family, he spent much of his adult life in Rome, where he was an active member of a circle of young poets whose urbane and expressive writings earned them the label of "new poets." Though well-regarded during his lifetime, Catullus' poems were lost for centuries before a copy of them resurfaced in Verona, his hometown, in the late 13th century.

PAUL CELAN

Paul Celan was born in Czernowitz, the capital of the Bukovina (now part of the Ukraine and Rumania), in 1920, to a Jewish family. In 1940 Soviet troops occupied his home town, only to be replaced by Rumanian and German Nazi troops the next year. Celan worked in forced labor camps, where, in the fall of 1942, he learned that his father had been killed by the SS. Later that winter the news reached him that his mother too had been shot. In 1947, he clandestinely crossed over to Vienna, which he left in 1948 to settle in Paris, the city that was to be his home until his suicide by drowning in the Seine in April 1970. Among Celan's major writings are *Mohn und Gedächtnis* (1952), *Die Niemandsrose* (1963), *Atemwende* (1967), and *Lichtzwang* (1970).

ANGEL CRESPO

Angel Crespo (1926–1995) was born in La Mancha and died in Barcelona. He wrote over 50 books of poetry and translation, and numerous works of criticism. He was labeled a traitor under Spain's Franco regime for signing a petition to protest the torture of miners in Asturias. Afterwards, he participated in clandestine antigovernment activities until he was eventually driven into exile. Crespo is one of Spain's most significant poets and translators of the 20th century; in fact, one of Spain's most prestigious prizes for translation, the Premio de Traducción Ángel Crespo, is awarded annually in Barcelona.

MICHEL DEGUY

Michel Deguy, a leading contemporary French poet and intellectual, was born in Paris in 1930. He is Editor-in-chief of the quarterly journal *PO&SIE* and Professor Emeritus, Université de Paris VIII. In 1989, he received the Grand Prix National de Poésie and began his term as president of the Collège International de Philosophie (through 1992). Among his 38 book publications since the first volume, *Les Meurtrières* (1959), are the following recent titles: *Gisants: Poèmes 1980–1995*, *L'Impair* (2001), and *Un homme de peu de foi* (2002).

NUALA NÍ DHOMNHAILL

Nuala Ní Dhomnhaill was born in Lancashire, England in 1952 to Irish-speaking parents. She grew up in West Kerry and in Tipperary. Her recent books include *The Water Horse* (Wake Forest Univ. Press, 1999), *Cead Aighnis* (An Sagart, 1998), and *The Astrakhan Cloak* (Wake Forest, 1993). Last year she was named as the second Ireland Professor of Poetry.

JEAN-MICHEL ESPITALLIER

Jean-Michel Espitallier is an editor of the influential French periodical *JAVA*. He lives in Paris.

LEA GOLDBERG

Lea Goldberg was born in Königsburg, East Prussia (now Kaliningrad, Russia), and settled in Tel Aviv in 1935. Apart from poetry and literary criticism, she wrote numerous books for children and translated European classics into Hebrew. She died in 1970, and is widely regarded as one of the leading poets of her time.

NAZIM HİKMET

Nazım Hikmet (1902–1963) was Turkey's most important modern poet. He graduated from Moscow's Workers of the East University. As a lifelong communist, he spent many years in prison and in exile. In addition to a massive corpus of poetry, he published novels, essays, and translations. His poetry has been translated into dozens of languages.

KAREL HLAVÁČEK

Karel Hlaváček was a leading poet in the Czech Symbolist and Decadence movements. *A Vengeful Cantilena*, first published in 1898, is a cycle of 12 poems and is considered to be the centerpiece of Hlaváček's poetic oeuvre. The poem's subject matter is a hybrid of two unrelated sources: the novel *Manon Lescaut*, a moral tale about the wasted life of a talented young French aristocrat who leaves seminary to pursue Manon, a woman of dubious character, and the violent uprising of the Gueux, a 16th century Dutch revolutionary group, against Spanish Catholic rule.

FRIEDRICH HÖLDERLIN

Friedrich Hölderlin (1770–1843) studied theology at Tübingen seminary, where met Hegel and Schelling. He began writing poetry in his teens and occasionally published in anthologies. In 1797, he published the first volume of an epistolary novel, *Hyperion*. In 1799, he planned a "humanistic magazine," *Iduna*, but could not find any contributors. In 1802 he had a mental breakdown, but kept on writing. His first book of poetry was compiled by friends in 1826.

HWANG JI-WOO

Hwang is professor and chair of the Department of Playwriting at the Korean National University of Arts. He led a new wave of deconstructionist poetry in the 1980's, which was part of the new "rhetoric of resistance" in Korean literature. He is the author of six poetry collections, among them *Even the Birds Leave the World* (1983), *A Lotus in the Crab's Eye* (1990), *I'll Sit Alone in a Darkened Pub* (1998), and four plays. His study of aesthetics and art history at Seoul National University was interrupted by a forced enlistment in the army following his imprisonment for student activism against the military dictatorship. His work has received numerous national awards.

HÉDI KADDOUR

Hédi Kaddour was born in Tunisia in 1945, but has lived in France since childhood. He has published three books of poems with Gallimard: *La Fin des vendanges* (1989), *Jamais une ombre simple* (1994), and *Passage au Luxembourg* (2000), as well as three books with smaller publishers, and a collection of essays on poetry, *L'Emotion impossible*. He lives in Paris, and teaches at L'Ecole Normale Supérieure in Lyon. Other poems of his, in Marilyn Hacker's translation, have appeared in *APR*, *The New Yorker*, *The Paris Review*, *Poetry*, *Prairie Schooner*, and *Verse*, as well as in the Faber anthology, *Twentieth Century French Poems*.

ABDELLATIF LAÂBI

Abdellatif Laâbi, founder of the magazine *Souffles*, spent eight years in prison in his native Morocco as a result of his work with the Association de Recherche Culturelle. Now living in France, he continues to write in many genres, especially poetry, and to work toward a world where writers do not think of themselves as citizens of a particular country.

LÂM THỊ MỸ DẠ

Lâm Thị Mỹ Dạ lives in Hue, Vietnam. She has worked as a reporter and a literary editor. She has published five collections of poems and three books for children, and has won several major prizes for poetry. Translations of her poems have been featured in *Six Vietnamese Poets* (Curbstone, 2002), and a bilingual collection of her poems translated by Martha Collins and Thuy Dinh will be published by Curbstone.

RADMILA LAZIC

Radmila Lazic (b. 1949) is one of the best living Serbian poets. She is the author of six collections of poetry and has published numerous essays on literature. She was the founder and editor of the journal *Profemina*, and had edited anthologies of women's poetry and of anti-war letters. The poem in this issue is among the first of her poems translated into English.

LI PO

Li Po (707–762) is without doubt the best-known Chinese poet. The Chinese share the title of "Greatest Poet" between Tu Fu, "the greatest *human* poet" and Li Po, "the spirit of poetry incarnate."

FRANCO LOI

Franco Loi was born in Genova in 1930, and moved to Milan at the age of seven. The poems in *Secundum Lüna* date from 1965, but they were published in 1975 as the final chapter in *Strölegh*. Since then, Loi has published 14 other books of poetry, as well as a number of translations and works of literary criticism. Loi's choice to write in Milanese dialect, an adopted, anti-literary language, is partly a choice to bring music, and the entirety of the human experience, back into the domain of poetry. He goes hunting for his poetry by night in local bars, and by day in public parks.

PURA LÓPEZ-COLOMÉ

Pura López-Colomé was born in Mexico City in 1952. She is the author of several books including *Aurora* and *Musica Inaudita*. *No Shelter* (2002), a collection of her poems translated by Forrest Gander, was published by Graywolf. A literary critic and translator, she has rendered into Spanish major works by H.D., Virginia Woolf, Gertrude Stein, Samuel Beckett, and Robert Hass. She lives in Cuernavaca, Mexico.

SAHIR LUDHYANVI

See page 178.

MENG HAO-JAN

Meng Hao-jan (689–740 C.E.), esteemed elder to a long line of China's greatest poets, was the first to make poetry from the Ch'an (Zen) Buddhist insight that deep understanding lies beyond words. The result was a strikingly distilled language that made Meng Hao-jan China's first master of the short imagistic landscape poem that came to typify ancient Chinese poetry. The translations in this issue are from the forthcoming (Jan. 2004) *Mountain Poems of Meng Hao-jan* (Archipelago Books), which will be the first edition of Meng Hao-jan's work in English.

HENRI MICHAUX

A painter, journalist, and poet, Michaux (1899–1984) became one of France's foremost writers, despite his reclusive nature. Michaux was born in Belgium, but moved to Paris in 1923, and began to paint and contribute to avant-garde reviews soon afterward. He traveled widely throughout North and South America, Asia, and Africa, and documented his trips with several travelogues. He also experimented with mescaline; his work explored happiness and agony as states produced by the drug. In 1965 he refused to accept the Grand Prix Nationale des Lettres in protest against the practice of awarding such prizes. His principal works include *Un Certain Plume* (1930), *Passages* (1950), *Émergences-résurgances* (1972), and *Affrontements* (1986).

PAUL MORAND

Paul Morand (1884–1976) was a poet, fiction writer, essayist, and diplomat whose work was largely devoted to the variety of people and places in the world. Among his many books are *Arc Lights* (1919); *USA* (1927), from which the poems in this issue are excerpted; *Black Magic* (1928); *New York* (1929); *World Champions* (1930); and *Hecate and Her Dogs* (1954).

MYRIAM MOSCONA

Myriam Moscona was born in Mexico City in 1955. She has published six books of poetry, including *Negro marfil* (2000) and *Visperas*, (1996). She has translated Kenneth Rexroth and William Carlos Williams into Spanish, and she worked for many years as an anchorwoman on public televsion. Translations of her poems can be found in *Mouth to Mouth: Poems by Twelve Contemporary Mexican Women* (ed. Forrest Gander, Milkweed Editions, 1993), and in *Aufgabe* (2003).

SANDRA MOUSSEMPÈS

Sandra Moussempès was born in Paris in 1965. She is the author of three books of poetry, *Exercices d'incendie* (Fourbis, 1994), *Vestiges de fillette* (Flammarion, 1997), and *Hors champs* (CRL Franchecont, 2001), in which the poem in this issue appeared. Her next book, *Captures*, is forthcoming from Flammarion.

PABLO NERUDA

A Chilean poet, and diplomat, Pablo Neruda was awarded the Nobel Prize for Literature in 1971.

FRANCIS PICABIA

Francis Picabia (1879–1953), of Spanish descent on his father's side, is best known for his Dadaist/Surrealist paintings. His lesser-known writing fills a two-volume collection. "Cuvette" was first printed in the book *Fifty-Two Mirrors* (*Cinquante-Deux Miroirs*, 1917), written in part during his visit to New York City.

FRANCISCO DE QUEVEDO

Francisco de Quevedo (y Villegas) was born in Madrid in 1580. He studied to become a Jesuit priest, but in 1605 retreated to La Torre de Juan Abad. In 1639 he was arrested with no clear charges, except a rumor that he conspired with the French. He died in 1645, one year after being released from prison. His works were published posthumously by his friend Jose Gonzalez de Salas.

OKTAY RIFAT

Oktay Rifat (1914–1988) graduated from the Faculty of Law at Ankara University and served for many years as legal counsel for the Turkish State Railways. Rifat was one of the three major figures of the movement known as *Garip* (Strange) in the 1940's. From the mid-1950's onward he went through periods of obscurantism and philosophical verse. In addition to being one of Turkey's foremost modernists in poetry, he enjoyed renown as a playwright, novelist, and translator. He was honored with virtually all of Turkey's major literary awards.

ARTHUR RIMBAUD

Although his period of poetic output was furious and brief, Rimbaud's (1854–1891) influence is as lasting as his life is misunderstood. All of his poems were written by his twenty-second year, after which he turned his back on a literary world that has been chasing him ever since.

TOMASZ RÓŻYCKI

Tomasz Różycki, Polish poet and translator, was born in 1970. He has published four collections of poems: *Vaterland* (1997), *Anima* (1999), *Chata umaita* (2001), and *Świat i antyświat* (2003). His poems have been translated into German, French, Spanish, English, Russian, and Ukrainian, and they been published in anthologies in Bulgaria, Lithuania, and Germany. He lives in Opole, Poland.

AKUTAGAWA RYŪNOSUKE

Akutagawa Ryūnosuke was born in Tokyo in 1892. As a young man he began publishing the short stories that would eventually be collected in *Rashōmon*, making him one of modern Japan's most famous authors. He studied under two of the most visible literary masters of the day: Natsume Sōseki, a novelist, and Takahama Kyoshi, a haiku master of the mainstream school. He published his haiku under the penname *"Gaki"* ("Hungry Ghost"). Suffering from severe depression, he committed suicide in 1927, at the age of 36.

TOMAŽ ŠALAMUN

Tomaž Šalamun, a Slovenian poet, is at the moment living in Berlin as a writer in residence. His last books translated in English are *The Four Questions of Melancholy, Feast,* and *A Ballad for Metka Krasovec. Poker,* his first Slovenian samizdat book, from which these poems are taken, will be published by Ugly Duckling Press this Fall.

BENILDA SANTOS

Benilda Santos is currently Dean of the School of Humanities at Ateneo de Manila University. She has published three books of poetry, most recently *Alipato: Mga Bago at Piling Tula (Flying Embers: New and Selected Poems),* and has won several awards, including the Philippine National Book Award. The translation and poem in this issue will appear in an upcoming bilingual edition of her work.

SAPPHO

Sappho was a late 7th-early 6th C. BCE lyric poet from the isle of Lesbos, about whom little is known,though legends have of course proliferated. What we do know of Sappho: the fragments that have been preserved, their erotic intensity, her revered status in antiquity, and her ongoing fascination for moderns. She composed in her local Aeolic dialect, love-lyrics as well as epithalamia which may have been sung at actual weddings. Among her songs are lyrics set in repeated stanzas of four lines, a form now called "Sapphic."

LÉOPOLD SÉDAR SENGHOR

Léopold Sédar Senghor (1906–2001) founded the Négritude movement, an international movement of Francophone writers of African descent, with Aimé Césaire, Léon Damas, and others. He became the first president of Senegal after its independence, serving from 1960 to 1981. Throughout his life, he wrote, translated, and published poetry, receiving numerous awards, including the Grand Prix International de Poésie and the Prix de la Langue Française. Senghor was elected to the Académie Française in 1983, as the first (and still only) black writer to serve this prestigious institute of the French language.

TONE ŠKRJANEC

Tone Škrjanec was born in Ljubljana (Slovenia) in 1953. His books include *Blues of a Swing* (1997), *The Sun on a Knee* (1999), *Pagodas on Wind* (2001), and *Knives* (2002). He translates poems and novels from English, Croatian, and Serbian into Slovene.

MORTEN SØNDERGAARD

Morten Søndergaard, a Danish poet living in Tuscany, Italy, has published several books of poetry. He was awarded the Martin Strunge Award in 1998. In 2002, his most recent collection was shortlisted for the Nordic Council's Literature Award, the largest and most prestigious award for Nordic literature.

FERNANDO SÁNCHEZ SORONDO

Fernando Sánchez Sorondo is the author of numerous poetry and short story collections and four novels. In 1963, he won the biannual Argentinean National Literature Award for his story collection *Por Orden de Azar.* He writes frequently for the Argentinean press and works as a speech writer for the Argentinean Department of the Exterior.

JOAQUIM DE SOUSÂNDRADE

Born and raised in the Northeast of Brazil, the poet Joaquim de Sousândrade (1833–1902) traveled widely and was educated in Europe. In 1871, he came to New York City, where he composed *O Guesa Errante (The Wandering Guesa).* His highly innovative poetry never received the attention of his contemporaries, and he died impoverished, selling, or as he reported, "eating" the stones of his landed estate, in order to survive.

TAKARABE TORIKO

Takarabe was born in Niigata in 1933, and shortly thereafter moved to Manchuria. Following the Soviet invasion of Manchuria and Japan's defeat in August 1945, all 320,000 Japanese immigrants became refugees. Takarabe's father and sister died in the chaos and deprivation that followed. It took 13 months for the remaining family to return to Japan. Takarabe published her first book of poems, *Watashi ga Kodomo datta Koro (When I was a Child),* in 1965. Among her other books are *Saiyūki (Journey to the West,* 1984), and *Uyū no Hito (Nonexistent Person,* 1998). She translates modern Chinese poems.

ÜLKÜ TAMER

Ülkü Tamer (b. 1937) is an award winning poet, short-story writer, and translator. His scores of translations range from Euripides to Neil Simon, from Shakespeare to Brecht. He has also published numerous children's books and major anthologies. He is currently a weekly columnist for the newspaper *Milliyet.*

GEORG TRAKL

Georg Trakl (1887–1914) was Austrian. Trained as a pharmacist, he was passionately hyper-sensitive. Compelled to do military service in World War I, he found war's brutality completely unbearable and killed himself. "De Profundis" was written in 1912. "Lament," titled *"Klage"* in the original, is famously one of the very last two poems Trakl wrote.

KIRMEN URIBE

Kirmen Uribe is the author of *Bitartean heldu eskutik* (*Meanwhile Hold Hands*), which won Spain's 2001 Premio de la Crítica, and whose Spanish translation will be published this fall. His 2001 multimedia collaboration with the musician Mikel Urdangarin was made into *Bar Puerto*, a CD-book. Uribe lives in Vitoria-Gasteiz (Euskadi, Spain).

YÜAN MEI

Yüan Mei (1716–1798), feminist, democrat, gourmet, sensualist, and family man, was the most important literary man of 18th century China.

NURIT ZARHI

Nurit Zarhi was born in Jerusalem in 1941 and lives in Tel Aviv. She studied Literature and Philosophy at the University of Tel Aviv, and has worked as a journalist and a literary critic. Her poems have been widely translated and anthologized in Europe, and she is also one of Israel's best-known authors of children's books. She has published seven volumes of poetry and received every major Israeli award.

Translators

ALAN B. ABRAMSON

Alan B. Abramson lives in New York City with his wife, two sons, and a Welsh Terrier whose ancestors hunted varmints to commands spoken in Middle Gaelic. He is an ashtanga yoga practitioner.

KRISTEN ANDERSEN

A New Jersey native, Kristen Andersen now lives and writes in Colorado, where she is working towards an M.F.A. in Creative Writing-Translation at Naropa University. She co-edits the literary/artistic journal *Sliding Uteri: A Rebirth of Poetic Language.*

My particular favorite idiom in French is la petite mort. *Literally, it means "the little death"; idiomatically, it means orgasm. The idea of orgasm always being some small death, where we lose all sense of self and separateness, strikes me as both extraordinarily poetic and accurate.* La petite mort *also reminds me of the sanskrit* parasamgate, *which in the Heart Sutra (a key Buddhist teaching on wisdom, compassion, and enlightenment) refers to the dissolution of self in enlightenment as the same dissolution of self experienced in sexual ecstasy.*

WILSON BALDRIDGE

Wilson Baldridge is associate professor of French at Wichita State University. His articles on Deguy have appeared in *Symposium*, the *Cahier Michel Deguy*, *Modernités*, and other journals. His translation of Deguy's book of poems, *Recumbents*, is forthcoming from Wesleyan Univ. Press.

JOSHUA BECKMAN

Joshua Beckman is the author of three books of poetry and has a fourth, *Your Time Has Come*, due out in the spring from Verse Press. His translations of Tomaž Šalamun's first book, *Poker*, are due out from Ugly Duckling Press this Fall.

JENNY BOULLY

Jenny Boully's book *The Body* is out from Slope Editions, and other work can be found in *The Best American Poetry 2002*, *The Next America Essay*, and *Great American Prose Poems*.

OLIVIER BROSSARD

Olivier Brossard is a contributing editor for *Double Change*, a French-American translation collective and online magazine. He is co-editing an anthology of contemporary French poetry with Marcella Durand, Kristin Prevallet, and Omar Berrada for Talisman Publishing House.

MARY ANN CAWS

Mary Ann Caws is Distinguished Professor of English, French, and Comparative Literature at the Graduate Center, City University of New York. Her recent publications include *Picasso's Weeping Woman: the Life and Art of Dora Maar* (2000), and *Robert Motherwell with Pen and Brush* (2003). She edited *The Surrealist Painters and Poets* (2001), *Manifesto: A Century of Isms* (2001), and edited and co-translated *The Yale Book of Twentieth Century French Poetry*, forthcoming in Spring.

> *My favorite expression is deeply André Breton:* jusqu'a nouvel ordre.... *which looks forward to everything changing, as surrealism meant it to.*

GIULIANA CHAMEDES

Giuliana Chamedes was born in New York City. She has published in the *Vermont Literary Review* and translated the poetry of Milli Graffi (Burning Deck Press, 2002). She is currently completing a Masters in History at the University of Cambridge.

> *There is a word in Milanese dialect,* strabeless, *for the drop of wine that remains at the bottom of the glass that you've bought at the bar; a drop that poor men, unable to afford a glass of wine, wander from table to table and drink.*

HAMIDA BANU CHOPRA

Hamida Banu Chopra taught Urdu language and literature at the University of California, Berkeley. She is a renowned reciter of Urdu poetry and has appeared at *mushairas* (poetry gatherings) in the U.S., Canada, and India. Two cassettes of her reading Urdu poetry have been recorded under the titles *Parinda Ki Faryad (The Bird's Plea)* and *Banjara (Gypsy)*. Her co-translations from Urdu of poetry by Faiz Ahmed Faiz and Sahir Ludhyanvi have appeared in *Two Lines*.

NASREEN G. CHOPRA

Nasreen G. Chopra is an experimental physicist who obtained a Ph.D. in Physics from the University of California, Berkeley. Her co-translation of a poem by Faiz Ahmed Faiz appeared in *Two Lines*.

ODILE CISNEROS

Odile Cisneros is a critic, writer and translator from Mexico, currently living in Edmonton, Alberta, Canada. Her translations and essays have been published in *Sibila* (Brazil), *Poesía y poética* (Mexico), *Sibila* (Spain), *Ecopoetics*, and *Chain*. She has translated the poetry of Régis Bonvicino, Haroldo de Campos, Rodrigo Rey Rosa, and Jaroslav Seifert. The translation in this issue will appear in *500 Years of Latin American Poetry*, forthcoming from Oxford Univ. Press.

PETER COLE

Peter Cole's most recent book of poetry is *Hymns & Qualms*. He has published many volumes of translations from contemporary and medieval Hebrew and Arabic, and has received numerous awards for his work, including the MLA Translation Prize for *Selected Poems of Shmuel HaNagid* and a Guggenheim Fellowship. He lives in Jerusalem.

BILLY COLLINS

Billy Collins is the author of several books of poetry, including *Nine Horses; Sailing Alone Around the Room: New and Selected Poems; Picnic, Lightning*; and *The Art of Drowning*. His was previously Poet Laureate of the United States, and he is a professor of English at Lehman College, City University of New York.

MARTHA COLLINS

Martha Collins' most recent collection of poems is *Some Things Words Can Do*. Her co-translations of poems by Vietnamese poet Nguyen Quang Thieu, *The Women Carry River Water*, won an award from the American Literary Translators Association. She teaches creative writing at Oberlin College.

THUY DINH

Thuy Dinh is a writer and attorney who has lived in Washington, D.C. since 1975. Her essays and reviews have appeared in *Rain Taxi, Hop Luu Magazine, Amerasia Journal*, and *Twenty Years of Vietnamese American Experience*.

SHARON DOLIN

Sharon Dolin's second book, *Serious Pink*, has just been published by Marsh Hawk Press and another collection, *Realm of the Possible*, will be published by Four Way Books in 2004. Poems of hers have recently appeared or are forthcoming in *American Letters & Commentary, Denver Quarterly, Tin House, Pool, Crowd, The Kenyon Review, Drunken Boat*, and *580 Split*.

CLAYTON ESHLEMAN

In 2001 Wesleyan University Press published Aimé Césaire's *Notebook of a Return to the Native Land*, co-translated by Clayton Eshleman and Annette Smith; in 2000 the same press brought out Eshleman's translation of Cesar Vallejo's *Trilce*.

LARA GLENUM

Glenum is an assistant editor of *Verse*, and her own poems have appeared or are forthcoming in *Fence, 3rd Bed*, and *The Black Warrior Review*, among others.

PAMELA GREENBERG

Pamela Greenberg's poetry has appeared in the *Missouri Review, Green Mountain Review, Shankpainter*, and elsewhere. She teaches at Bunker Hill Community College.

JACEK GUTOROW

Jacek Gutorow (b. 1970) has published three books of poems, a book of essays on Derrida's deconstruction, and a collection of essays on the Polish poets after 1968. He is working on a monograph of Wallace Stevens and teaches at the University of Opole.

MARILYN HACKER

Marilyn Hacker is the author of ten books, including the just-published *Desesperanto*. Her other books include *Winter Numbers*, *Selected Poems*, *Squares and Courtyards*, and *She Says*, a translated collection of Vénus Khoury-Ghata's poems published by the Graywolf Press. She lives in New York and Paris, and teaches at the City College of New York.

GORDON HADFIELD

Gordon Hadfield is a poet and a student in the Buffalo Poetics Program. Recent work has appeared in *Ribot*, *Interim*, and *Ecopoetics*.

NANCY HADFIELD

Nancy Hadfield teaches British Medieval and Renaissance literature at Central Methodist College in Fayette, Missouri.

TALAT S. HALMAN

Talat S. Halman is a poet, literary critic, and professor. He has taught Turkish language, literature and culture at Columbia, Princeton, and NYU. Currently he is Chairman of the Department of Turkish Literature at Bilkent University (Ankara). He has published more than 50 books and numerous articles in English and Turkish. In 1971 he served as Turkey's Minister of Culture and in the early 1980's as Ambassador for Cultural Affairs.

One of my favourite expressions in Turkish is saçını süpürge etmek (literally "to make one's hair a broom"), with its evocation of a virtually surrealistic image, meaning "To exert oneself to be of service, to do one's utmost to help someone." To translate it and to do justice to it is extremely difficult.

DAVID HINTON

David Hinton's many translations of ancient Chinese poetry have earned wide acclaim. He is the first in over a century to translate the four originary masterworks of Chinese philosophy: *Tao Te Ching, Chuang Tzu, Analects*, and *Mencius*. His many awards include a Guggenheim Fellowship and grants from the NEA and the NEH. Hinton's poem-map, *Fossil Sky*, is forthcoming this spring from Archipelago Books. He lives in East Calais, Vermont.

JEN HOFER

Jen Hofer is the editor and translator of *Sin puertas visibles: An Anthology of Contemporary Poetry by Mexican Women* (Univ. of Pittsburgh Press and Ediciones Sin Nombre, 2003), and the author of *slide rule* (subpress, 2002). Her poems, prose texts, and translations can be found in recent issues of *26, A.BACUS, Conundrum, Enough, kiosk*, and *Aufgabe*.

I am consistently enamored of the phrase por si las moscas, *which literally means "for if the flies" and is used when you need a little extra something,* por si las moscas—*just in case.*

JOSEF HORÁČEK

Josef Horáček is a native of the Czech Republic who currently resides in Athens, GA. In 2000, he and his wife, Lara Glenum, received a Fulbright grant to live in Prague and translate Czech Symbolist poetry. They are currently translating Czech avant-garde poets.

CHRISTINE HUME

Christine Hume is the author of *Musca Domestica* (Beacon, 2000) and *Alaskaphrenia* (New Issues, 2004). She teaches at Eastern Michigan University.

JOHN IRONS

John Irons (b. 1942) studied French, German and Dutch literature at Cambridge University, where he also gained his Ph.D. He has translated a wide range of Dutch, Flemish, and Scandinavian poetry, including such Danish poets as Henrik Nordbrandt, Klaus Høeck, and Inger Christensen.

ANA JELNIKAR

Ana Jelnikar was born in Ljubljana in 1975. She is currently working towards an M.A. in English Literature at the Open University (England). Her translations of Slovenian poets have appeared in *Verse, Southern Humanities Review, Third Coast*, and *The American Poetry Review*. She is also the translator of the first Slovenian edition of C. G. Jung's *Man and His Symbols*.

FAITH JONES

Faith Jones is a short-story writer, translator, and researcher. Her work has been published in *Lyric, Bridges, Fiddlehead*, and *Geist*, and in the anthology *Beautiful as the Moon, Radiant as the Stars* (Warner Books). She is a librarian in the Dorot Jewish Division of the New York Public Library.

PIERRE JORIS

Pierre Joris left Luxembourg at 19, and has since lived in Great Britain, North Africa, France, and the U.S., where he now teaches poetry & poetics at SUNY Albany. Recent books include *Poasis: Selected Poems 1986–1999*, and *A Nomad Poetics* (essays). Recent books of translation include *4 x 1: Work by Tristan Tzara, Rainer Maria Rilke, Jean-Pierre Duprey & Habib Tengour* and Abdelwahab Meddeb's *The Malady of Islam*. In 2004 Green Integer will reissue three volumes of his translations of Paul Celan: *Breathturn*, *Threadsuns*, and *Lightduress*.

JEFFREY JULLICH

Jeffrey Jullich's translations of Comte Robert de Montesquiou's poetry have been published in *The Transcendental Friend*, of Victor Hugo's ouija board-dictated poetry in *litvert*, and other Picabia translations are forthcoming in the Paris-based *Upstairs at Duroc*. His own writing has been published in *Fence, Shiny, American Letters & Commentary, Poetry,* etc.

> The on-line list of French idioms, which offers the French idiom, une capote anglaise (an "English bonnet" or "hood"), translates it into English with the English idiom, "a French letter." Strange semantic international waters, where "English" means "French": I knew neither the word capote (as in Truman Capote?) nor the meaning of "French letter" before checking dictionaries, a dictionary-checking that left me feeling like a school boy searching for definitions of dirty words. Both idioms, it turns out, mean "condom."

TSIPI KELLER

Tsipi Keller's honors include an NEA Translation Fellowship and NYFA awards in fiction. Her translation of Dan Pagis's *Last Poems*, was published by *The Quarterly Review of Literature* (1993), and her translation of Irit Katzir's *And I Wrote Poems*, was published by Carmel (2000). Her novels include *The Prophet of Tenth Street* (1995), *Leverage* (1997), and the forthcoming *Jackpot* (Spuyten Duyvil, 2004).

WON-CHUNG KIM

Won-Chung Kim is currently a professor of English Literature at Sungkyunkwan University in Seoul, Korea. He earned his Ph.D. in English poetry at the University of Iowa. He has translated Chiha Kim's *Heart's Agony* (White Pine Press, 1998), Seungho Choi's *Flowers in the Toilet Bowl* (Homa & Sekey, 2003), and Hyonjong Chong's *Trees of the World* (Kegan Paul International, forthcoming), and will soon publish an anthology of Korean ecological poets.

LISA LUBASCH

Lisa Lubasch is the author of *To Tell the Lamp* (Avec Books, 2004), *Vicinities* (Avec, 2001), and *How Many More of Them Are You?* (Avec, 1999). She is the translator of Paul Eluard's *A Moral Lesson*, and is one of several editors of *Double Change*, an online journal dedicated to French-American interaction in poetry.

ELIZABETH MACKLIN

Elizabeth Macklin has published two collections of poems, *A Woman Kneeling in the Big City* and *You've Just Been Told*. In 1999–2000 she spent an Amy Lowell Poetry Traveling Scholarship year studying the Basque language in Bilbao, Spain. She is a freelance writer and editor in New York City.

> To say "blah-blah-blah"—or any similarly indefinite and irreverent quasi-quotation—in Castillian Spanish people say no sé qué, no sé cuántos: "I don't know what, I don't know how many." In Basque, though, what people say instead is ez dakit zer, badakit zer: "I don't know what, I do know what." The contrast somehow gives it the spin of a street-smart New Yorker's "yadda-yadda-yadda."

WYATT MASON

Wyatt Mason is a translator and critic. He is currently a fellow of the Dorothy and Lewis B. Cullman Center for Scholars and Writers of the New York Public Library where he is translating the essays of Michel de Montaigne.

MAUREEN N. MCLANE

Maureen N. McLane is a Visiting Scholar in the Comparative Media Studies Program at MIT. Her essays have recently appeared in *The New York Times, The Boston Review*, and *The Boston Globe*. Her poems have been featured in *New American Writing, jacket*, and *The Harvard Review*. Of her poems in this issue, she writes: "These poems (not translations exactly) are perhaps best considered aftermaths, afterimages, lyric transpositions—inflected by long sitting with the Loeb edition of Greek Lyric, vol. 1, English translation by David A. Campbell (Harvard Univ. Press, 1982), and more profoundly by repeated reading of Jim Powell's stunning *Sappho: A Garland* (Farrar Straus, 1993), whose Sappho is, until I learn Greek, my Sappho."

JOYELLE MCSWEENEY

Joyelle McSweeney's first book, *The Red Bird*, won the Fence Modern Poets Prize and was published in 2002 by Fence Books/Saturnalia Books. She teaches at the University of Alabama in Tuscaloosa.

CHRISTOPHER MERRILL

Christopher Merrill's books include four collections of poetry, *Brilliant Water, Workbook, Fevers & Tides*, and *Watch Fire*; translations of Aleš Debeljak's *Anxious Moments* and *The City and the Child*; several edited volumes; and three books of nonfiction, including *Only the Nails Remain: Scenes from the Balkan Wars*. His work has been translated into 12 languages. He directs the International Writing Program at The University of Iowa.

CHRIS MICHALSKI

Chris Michalski's translations from Spanish and German have appeared in journals in the U.S. and overseas. He has recently completed a new translation of Jose Eustasio Rivera's classic modernist novel, *La vorágine*.

RICK MOODY

Rick Moody is the author of the memoir *The Black Veil* and the short story collection *Demonology*. His novels include *Purple America*, *The Ice Storm*, and *Garden State*, which won the Pushcart Press Editors' Book Award.

PAUL MULDOON

Paul Muldoon was born in 1951 in Northern Ireland and now lives in New Jersey, where he teaches at Princeton University. His most recent book is *Moy Sand and Gravel* (2002), for which he was awarded the 2003 Pulitzer Prize for Poetry.

EILEEN MYLES

Eileen Myles' books include *Skies* (2001), *on my way* (2001), *Cool for You* (2000), and *Chelsea Girls* (1994). With Liz Kotz, she edited *The New Fuck You/adventures in Lesbian Reading*. Her writings appear in *Book Forum, Art in America, The Village Voice, The Nation, The Stranger, Index*, and *Nest*.

IDRA NOVEY

Idra Novey's poetry, translations, and prose have appeared in publications in both the U.S. and Chile, including *Poetry International, Review: Latin American Literature and Art, El Mercurio*, Chile's central newspaper, and *Voces Emergentes*, a poetry anthology published last year by a Chilean university press. She is currently the Poetry Editor of *Columbia: A Journal of Literature and Art*.

> One Chilean phrase that has caught my attention is *estar en otra*, *meaning to feel removed from a situation, usually a mental remove from something for which one was physically present. The general definition of this phrase is easy enough to translate, but what is harder to transport into English is the connotations it's accrued in post-Pinochet Chilean culture. After 16 years of dictatorship during which there was scarce opportunity to have a say in politics, estar en otra has also become an informal way of stating a sociopolitical remove from what's happening in the country.*

RON PADGETT

Ron Padgett's books include *Oklahoma Tough: My Father, King of the Tulsa Bootleggers*; *You Never Know*; *The Straight Line: Writings on Poetry and Poets*; and *New & Selected Poems*. He is the translator of Blaise Cendrars' *Complete Poems* and Guillaume Apollinaire's *Poet Assassinated and Other Stories*. In 2001 the French Ministry of Culture and Communication made him an Officier dans l'Ordre des Arts et des Lettres.

KRISTIN PREVALLET

Kristin Prevallet is currently co-editing an anthology of contemporary French-language poetry for Talisman House Publishers. Her translations have appeared in the *Chicago Review, The Germ*, and *Poetry New York*. A recent essay on translation appears on the *Rain Taxi* website.

SEAN PRICE

Sean Price studies philosophy and the Japanese language at University of Missouri-St. Louis. In his spare time, he enjoys reading, flying kites, learning piano, and translating Japanese poetry.

BURTON RAFFEL

Burton Raffel was born in 1928, in New York City. A university teacher, he has also been an editor and a Wall Street lawyer. He has published poetry, fiction, literary criticism, annotated volumes of Milton and Shakespeare, and dozens of translations. The most recent is a new version of Stendhal's *Le Rouge et le Noir*, published by Modern Library in 2003.

> The most poignant line, among all the poems I have translated, is by Chairil Anwar (1922–49), Indonesia's Dante—or Pushkin—or Shakespeare. In "Aku," "Me," he ends by declaring "Aku mau hidup seribu tahun lagi"—simple words which make a tremendous ringing, permanently unforgettable impact. After many many attempts (and four different published versions), I translate this (much less tremendously) as "I want to live another thousand years." Forty years ago I met an Indonesian engineer, in a Philadelphia garage—and he proudly quoted the line (in Indonesian, of course).

JOSÉ EDMUNDO OCAMPO REYES

José Edmundo Ocampo Reyes holds an M.F.A. from Columbia University, where he received an Academy of American Poets Prize.

> A common Filipino expression is *kaing karpintero*, which is roughly equivalent to "eating as heartily as a carpenter." To help get them through their daily grind, carpenters and other manual laborers in the Philippines consume heavy amounts of rice relative to ulam (fish, meat, vegetables, or shrimp paste). For many Filipinos, including myself, rice has, in effect, become the main course, and ulam the side dish.

FLÁVIA ROCHA

Flávia Rocha is a Brazilian journalist, poet, and translator living in New York City. She is an editor for *Rattapallax* magazine, and an M.F.A. candidate in Poetry at Columbia University. In Brazil, she worked as a staff reporter and writer for magazines *Bravo!* and *Casa Vogue*, among others.

Se correr o bicho pega, se ficar o bicho come.—*"Run and the beast catches you, stay and the beast eats you." In this humorous and pessimistic proverb, there is no way out of the horrendous situation. Death will be certain and certainly painful. Bicho, a difficult world to translate, is very colloquial in Brazil. Used in slang, it can mean "brother." My dictionary gives the following: 1. any animal, excepting fowl and fish. 2. any insect that feeds on books. 3. ugly, repulsive or unsociable person. One of the most dangerous bichos on Earth is* Bicho-Papão, *who eats children if they are not obedient.*

ZACK ROGOW

Zack Rogow's fifth book of poems, *Greatest Hits: 1979–2001*, was published last year by Pudding House Publications. He is the editor of a new anthology of U.S. poetry, *The Face of Poetry*, to be published by Univ. of California Press in 2005. He translates French literature, and was a co-winner of the PEN/Book-of-the-Month Club Translation Award for *Earthlight* by André Breton. He teaches in the Writing Program at the California College of the Arts.

CECILIA ROHRER

Cecilia Rohrer attended the University of Michigan and the University of Oklahoma. She lives in Minneapolis and is Matthew's mother.

MATTHEW ROHRER

Matthew Rohrer is the author of *A Hummock in the Malookas, Satellite, Nice Hat. Thanks.* (with Joshua Beckman), and the forthcoming *A Green Light.*

HIROAKI SATO

Columnist, poet, and leading translator of Japanese poetry into English, Hiroaki Sato received the 1982 PEN American Center translation prize for *From the Country of Eight Islands: An Anthology of Japanese Poetry* (Doubleday, 1981; with Burton Watson). He writes the monthly column, "The View from New York," for *The Japan Times.* Among his most recent books are *Howling at the Moon: Poems and Prose of Hagiwara Sakutarō* (Green Integer, 2002) and *My Friend Hitler and Other Plays of Yukio Mishima* (Columbia Univ., 2002).

ANDREW SCHELLING

Andrew Schelling is a poet, ecology activist, and translator. He teaches poetry and Sanskrit at Naropa University in Colorado. A collection of essays from La Alameda Press, *Wild Form, Savage Grammar*, is his most recent book. Shambhala Publications will bring out his translation of the *Amarusataka*'s 101 poems in 2004.

J. P. SEATON

J. P. Seaton's translations have been widely anthologized. His most recent books include *I Don't Bow to Buddha*, selected poems of Yüan Mei, (Copper Canyon, 1997) and, to celebrate his recent retirement as Professor of Chinese at the University of North Carolina, a booklet of poems from the Zen recluse-poet Han Shan (Longhouse, 2003).

C. M. SHIPMAN

C. M. Shipman holds degrees in Celtic from the University of Oxford and Harvard University where she is currently working towards a Ph.D. in the Department of Celtic Languages and Literatures.

CHARLES SIMIC

Charles Simic was born in Belgrade in 1938. He received the Pulitzer Prize for *The World Doesn't End*, as well as a Guggenheim Foundation Scholarship and a MacArthur Foundation Fellowship. He is a professor of English at the University of New Hampshire. *A Wake for the Living*, his translations of Radmila Lazic's poems, is forthcoming from Graywolf Press.

RICK SNYDER

Rick Snyder's translations of Catullus' poems 1–30, *This Charming New Chapbook*, appeared earlier this year on Situations, and his essay on recent translations of Paul Celan appeared in *Radical Society.* His e-chapbook *Forecast Memorial* can be found on the Duration web site.

SAM STARK

Stark's translations and adulturations have appeared in *3rd bed*, on *McSweeney's Internet Tendency*, and *UbuWeb*.

STEVEN J. STEWART

Steven J. Stewart's poems and translations appear in numerous publications, including *Harper's, Seneca Review, Crazyhorse, jubilat, Hotel Amerika,* and *Poetry Daily.* His book of translations of Spanish poet Rafael Pérez Estrada is forthcoming from Hanging Loose Press in 2003. He is currently finishing a book-length manuscript of translations of Crespo's work.

In Spanish, salir el tiro por la culata, *means "to backfire," an expression which literally refers to a shot coming out through the butt of the gun. This phrase comes to mind because of a clever way I once saw it used in a translation. In an episode of* The Simpsons, *Bart has misbehaved in Australia and is about to be "booted," kicked in the rear end by a government official. At the last minute, Bart avoids the boot and moons the angry Australian onlookers. In the translated version of the episode I saw in Spain, Bart says of the failed booter,* Le ha salido el culo por la tirata, *switching* cul *with* tir, *making the butt of a gun into his own butt, wonderfully rendering a mooning as well as a backfiring. This is an example of how an astute translator and a little serendipity can make for an incredibly apt (and funny) translation.*

JASON STUMPF

Jason Stumpf's poems and reviews have recently appeared in *Boston Review* and *Pleiades.* He is Co-Director of Underwood Poetry, a non-profit literary organization in St. Louis.

GENE TANTA

Gene Tanta's writing has appeared in *Exquisite Corpse* and *Ploughshares,* among other publications. Currently, he lives in Chicago, where he teaches at Roosevelt University and Columbia College. Tanta also creates visual works with mixed-media of stolen valuables, so watch the little ones.

În America, umblâ câinii cu covrigi în coadâ.— *"In America, dogs walk around with cracknel baker (a hard, thin, and salted bread twisted in bow shape and baked golden) round their tails." This expresses the irony (or cynicism) felt by Romanians toward the naive expectations of their less traveled that assume that in America (or elsewhere) one need not to work to earn a living. This would be the sarcastic equivalent of: "There are no free lunches." Usually uttered as an immigrant's complaint to a native Romanian. This quick, economic, clean, tasty, and visually appealing snack is a staple element in the diet of urban Romanians on the run. It goes quite well with drinkable yogurt (and unregulated exhaust fumes).*

PATRICIA TERRY

Patricia Terry has taught French and Comparative Literature at Barnard College and at the University of California, San Diego. Her translations of medieval texts include *The Song of Roland* and *Renard the Fox.* She is also the co-author of *The Finding of the Grail: Retold from Old French Sources.* With John Ashbery and Mary Ann Caws she translated the *Selected Poems* of Pierre Reverdy.

EDWIN TORRES

Edwin Torres lives and works in New York City. He has traveled many landscapes, creating interdisciplinary performances. His work includes *The All-Union Day Of The Shock Worker* (Roof Books), *Fractured Humorous* (subpress), and *Holy Kid* (Kill Rock Stars, CD).

SUSAN WHEELER

Susan Wheeler is the author of three collections of poetry, *Source Codes, Smokes,* and *Bag 'o' Diamonds.*

DARA WIER

Dara Wier's most recent books are *Hat on a Pond* (Verse, 2002) and *Voyages In English* (Carnegie Mellon, 2001); her poems have been featured in 2003 in *American Poetry Review* and *Poetry Miscellany.* She lives in Amherst, Massachusetts where she teaches at the University of Massachusetts.

BILL ZAVATSKY

Bill Zavatsky has published two books of poetry and two books of translation—*The Poems of A.O. Barnabooth* by Valery Larbaud (with Ron Padgett) and *Earthlight,* poems by André Breton (with Zack Rogow). The latter will be reprinted in January of 2004 by Green Integer. *Earthlight* won the PEN/Book-of-the-Month-Club Translation Prize in 1993.

I've always loved that dopey expression, C'est la vie, *which is maybe the first French idiom that I learned. A friend and I used to joke by exclaiming (in English) to one another, about almost anything, "It is the life!" Is this expression the equivalent of our "That's life!" or would "That's how it goes!" be a better translation? Search me!*

David S. Allee   Kathleen Andersen   Ky Anderson   Robert Archambeau Mary Jo Bang Edward Bartok-Baratta Joshua Beckman John Beer Debbie Benson   Walead Beshty   Beth Block   Laure-Anne Bosselaar Jenny Boully Joe Brainard Pam Brown   Rafael Campo Jennifer Chang   Anna Collette Billy Collins   Shanna Compton   Kevin Cooley Michael Costello Jason Danzinger Sarah Darpli Cort Day Connie Deanovich Albert Flynn DeSilver Geoffrey Detrani Trane Devore Ray

ART ESSAYS FICTION PHOTOGRAPHY POETRY

DiPalma Sharon Dolin Brady Dollarhide Wei Dong Mary Donnelly Denise Duhamel Richard Dupont   Corwin Ericson George J Farrah MK Fancisco Jay Gardner Amy Gerstler John Gossage Arielle Greenberg Carl Gunhouse Jane Hammond Kristen Hanlon Harrison Haynes Lyn Hejinian Steven A Heller Alexander Heilner Alex Heminway Stephen Hilger   Shannon Holman   Henry Israeli   Shelley Jackson   Christopher

C R O W D

Kelty   Lisa Kereszi Barbara Kruger   Christine Kuan   Debora Kuan Susan Landers John Latta Brett Fletcher Lauer David Dodd Lee David Lehman Ben Lerner Luljeta Lleshanaku Timothy Liu Joyelle McSweeney Richard Meier Lynn Melnick Charlotte Mew Toni Mirosevich Matthew Monteith Nick Montfort Malena Morling Paul Muldoon Ryan Murphy Geoffrey G. O'Brien Kathleen Ossip Ron Padgett Danielle Pafunda Ethan Paquin Hyun-Doo Park Christa Parravani Chris Prentice Richard Prince David

487 UNION ST #3 BROOKLYN NY 11231

WWW.CROWDMAGAZINE.COM

Prete Kathryn Rantala Julie Reid Andrew Rodgers Andy Ryan Mark Salerno Maureen Seaton Ravi Shankar Steven Sherrill Lori Shine Amy Sillman Sean Singer Hugh Steinberg AL Steiner Virgil Suarez Derek Stroup Cole Swensen James Tate Matthew Thorburn David Todd Wells Tower Laura Gail Tyler Michael Vahranwald Kara Walker Clay Weiner Timothy Westmoreland Susan Wheeler Sam White Marina Wilson Ofer Wolberger Rebecca Wolff Matthew Zapruder Rachel Zucker